A Sacred Rage

A Sacred Rage

The Path of Constructive Conscience

Rev. John Simmons

To order additional copies of this book, contact:
Xlibris Corporation
1-888-795-4274
www.Xlibris.com
Orders@Xlibris.com
52035

Contents

*This book is dedicated
to all people in the hope of Partnership.*

There are many individuals significant on my path.

*A special acknowledgement
to Annamarie Midtlyng-Jackson—
my partner in sharing in this volume
the path of my life's ministry.*

CHAPTER ONE

Out of My Head

I was born on a chicken farm on May 20, 1917, in Mountain Grove, Missouri. My parents were John and Anna Groh Simmons. Of course nobody can know as much of their earliest childhood as they would like. How did my father end up living in Missouri for that short time? It intrigued me all my life, and I never found out what happened. I grew up in Iowa. I know what I learned of my family as I grew, a family that would shape my controversial ministry.

My family background was very unusual. My father was John Simmons. His parents both passed on by the time I came into this world. His mother died when he was only nine (that same year my father started working in a coal mine). His father was killed later in a hunting accident. My father never let me near a gun.

My mother was Anna Groh Simmons. Her father, Leonard Groh, was a Lutheran minister. His first wife, Martha Schruck Hicks, died at the age of thirty-six. His second wife (who was a Quaker from Quakertown, Pennsylvania, and sister of his first wife) died at the age of thirty-nine. He also laid to rest early his children, a son who lost his life in Central America in missionary enterprise and a daughter who succumbed to cancer in her thirties. He suffered personally from tuberculosis. Yet my grandfather never lost faith. After the death of his second wife, he said, "The Lord in His amazing kindness has met me round every corner."

My grandfather was the first preacher in Boyertown, Pennsylvania, to preach in German and English. That was tolerance in action during those days. Later he preached at St. Mark's Lutheran in Omaha, Nebraska. My grandfather also served for eight years on the board of trustees of Muhlenberg College. The Muhlenbergs were Lutherans. Henry Melchior Mühlenberg was founder of the Lutheran Church of America (LCA). They were also historically political. Frederick was a leader in the Continental Congress. A later Frederick Muhlenberg was a U.S. congressman. My grandfather publicly supported the candidacy of William Jennings Bryan, a Nebraskan, introducing him many times at public speeches in Lincoln and Omaha (preachers did not cross into politics at all then).

My uncle Eulalius was a man of God in the true sense of the word. He decided to preach the Gospel in Latin America—Guatemala, Mexico, and Honduras. His name means "of pleasing speech." He was truly unconcerned with worldly things—politics and money—just preaching the Gospel and saving souls. He didn't want an organization to support him, but rather to go as Jesus and the disciples went with only the support of God.

Finally there was my uncle Abraham Groh. He was an editor of the *Omaha Bee* and the *World Herald*, and he wrote articles for the *Saturday Evening Post*. He made oodles in stocks and lived in Beverly Hills with his wife, Nata (who was a member of the Church of Christian Science). I had a good correspondence with my uncle for many years. We would visit when I relocated to Southern California later in my life.

Myself at a young age

One of my childhood memories is our regular Sunday. Every Sunday, my mother took my brothers, Leonard and Robert; my sister, Jeannette; and me on the streetcar to Des Moines. It was thirty miles round trip (in those days, even nine miles was a hardship)! My mother did not like the local Lutheran pastor. She was familiar with Pastor Frederick Wertz at St. John's Lutheran in Des Moines. So every Sunday, church and Sunday school was the biggest part of our day. My father did not join us.

My father was not irreligious, but he was fairly critical of the preachers in our town. In his experience, the clergy and congregational leaders were always on the side of companies and the government. He was a labor organizer for the Switchman's Union of America. In the early 1920s, there was a railroad strike where we lived in Valley Junction, Iowa. Valley Junction was so named because it housed the switching facilities and repair shops for Chicago, Rock Island and Pacific Railroad. Most people worked for the railroad making the strike of 1922 against the railroads divisive. Workers and their children were called scabs if they worked during the strike. In a small town of 1,200, it was devastating to all. I remember my father would reprimand me if I ever spoke negatively of children whose fathers were not part of the union even though the relationship between children of scabs and not-scabs was a difficult one at play and at church.

When the strike was over, the railroad company began a campaign for every switchman to buy a home in Valley Junction, attracting all sorts of people to the neighborhood from black to Chicano to Italian. They wanted a stable union of employees. We bought a house at 516 Third Street—four blocks from the junction station and the switch shanty where all the switchmen met and did what they called chewing the fat. The language murdered the King's English!

My father told me of one meeting in downtown with the local Lutheran minister. (Remember, my mother had us travel quite a good distance as to NOT attend this particular Lutheran church). During the conversation, Dad used some of the "chewing the fat" language. The minister told Dad he shouldn't use those words. My dad said to him, "Reverend, you pray a lot and I swear a lot. Apparently neither of us means anything by it."

My dad made a good point! On the sixty-seventh anniversary of my ordination, May 7, 2009, I discovered a book by Jack Nelson-Pallmeyer called *Jesus Against Christianity: Reclaiming the Missing Jesus*. It helps me put into words the focus that was my ministry, the mystery of Jesus's disappearance from Christianity. The author in his introduction wrote, "I want to solve the case of Jesus' disappearance in order to make sense out of my life as a person of faith."

His words as to why the time is ripe for Jesus's return (to Christianity, not literally, of course): "Our world is falling apart under the collective weight of gross inequalities, massive injustice, violence, faulty definitions of life's meaning and distorted faith." And further, "The Christ of Faith enshrined in the creeds has literally displaced and rendered the life of Jesus meaningless."

Now, we live in a time in which the Gospel has been long lost in a life of the country, of the world. Someone tells me that he accepts Jesus as Lord and savior. I do too, but if it stops there, it isn't the Gospel! Jesus as my savior is missing from a religious model that continues to dominate. My duty is to live the same kind of life as Jesus—love for your enemies and all people without exception and without violence.

> Until you find the love you've missed you're nothing, Alfie.
> When you walk, let your heart lead the way
> And you'll find love any day, Alfie, Alfie
> would you tell me what's it all about?

These lyrics by Hal David and Burt Bacharach ask a question. My answer is another question: What does the Lord require of me? What is it all about, John? I have spent my lifetime trying to figure it out.

During my years in high school, I was a member of the debate team and the wrestling team. I wasn't a large kid to say the least, wrestling others in the 85 lb. to 95 lb. weight division. I was also the quarterback of the football team. The linemen were all farm boys. An article in the *Booster Express* said it best: "John had trouble seeing over the line of scrimmage."

My high school years were not easy years in this country. It was the time of the Depression. I know the ingenuity of the garden in the backyard—fruits, vegetables, chicken, and rabbits—essential for the family's survival. Mother made apple pies from two trees in the yard. The butcher gave liver and bones for free or a few cents.

My father had been elected as general chairman of the union. He was responsible for correspondence, difficult because he had lost two fingers on his right hand. When I entered the ninth grade, Dad asked if I would take shorthand and typing so I could help him. I did.

In 1935, I graduated from Valley Junction High School as class president. I went on to Drake University on a debate scholarship. Drake was known as a disciple college in that it trained Disciple of Christ ministers. Ronald Reagan went to one such school and nearly became a minister himself! While at Drake, I traveled the country with the dean of women driving the debate team. At Baylor University, an all-girl school, the local paper quoted me saying, "I have traveled from the Atlantic to the Pacific and never have I seen so much feminine pulchritude." At Stanford, I met the secretary of interior for Calvin Coolidge.

Times were still tough. I was only eighteen years old. In 1936, the railroad company my father worked for decided to move the junction to East Des Moines, nine miles from Valley Junction, without consulting the union. The railroad in Valley Junction moved the junction *after* convincing people to purchase property, making Valley Junction their permanent home. I helped my father who saw his town suffer in business and economic activity.

I have recently thought of similar situations when corporations have made ghost towns, disrupting the lives of the workers—Lockheed, Menasco, and Pacific Automotive, to name a few. If the town is lucky, it can recover over a span of years, but that is little consolation to the individuals affected by the loss of their work. I did some research and talked to Roger Babson, chief economist, about communities who had changed their names, such as Cleveland Heights. Babson said it was the best thing to happen to any of the towns that had done it. A movement was organized to change the name of the town to West Des Moines. The voters narrowly defeated it twice.

My father saw things a certain way—a community needs to step up to the plate when what was once in the community is suddenly gone. The name change could alter the damage done by the move of the railroad junction. There was a great significance to my father's "get up and do something" attitude. The name change was eventually won. West Des Moines is now one of the larger communities in Iowa. It is also the home of the Lutheran Church headquarters.

Everything about that time was difficult, but our home always welcomed large numbers of visitors. My mother was passionate about the church community, and my father cared about the social well-being of his larger family—humanity. He publicly supported Eugene Debs who rejected war and violence in any form. In addition to the name change, I worked on the first successful campaign of a Democratic congressman from Polk

County, Iowa, Hubert Utterback. I studied economics and political science at Drake.

While I was first at Drake University, I did more than study. I worked thirty hours a week at the Y with the Downtown Neighborhood Boys, or the DTN. The unemployment and poverty that followed the Depression made the YMCA a needed resource. I met people in leadership positions who taught me everything I needed for living a loving, creative life. (I was traveling with the debate team from Drake as well.)

In 1937, I was invited to perform in a church play (at St. John's) called *The Ring of Rama Krishna*. I began dating a young girl who was also in the play, Mary Jane. Mary Jane and I had been confirmed together. Back on campus, I was invited to join the top academic fraternity on campus—TEKE, or Tau Kappa Epsilon. (Ronald Reagan was a member of the fraternity!)

I graduated from Drake University in May 1939, an economics and philosophy major. I was selected by the faculty one of six graduates named outstanding leader. I had accumulated a number of honors, including an oratorical championship. Mary Jane was working for an insurance company. I worked for a lumber company in the summer. I didn't know what to do with my "outstanding leadership"—law school or seminary.

My father wanted to see me enter a law profession. My mom wanted me to pursue the ministry. Every person of religion has to decide how much religion influences life. I was becoming increasingly disturbed that the church was becoming more sectarian. I held radical views of what Christian people should be doing for justice; however, reflecting on my family history, I understood that law is not progressive. I entered Northwestern Lutheran Seminary in Minneapolis in 1939.

I had been active in a Luther League prior to entering seminary. The end of one particular Luther League camp was also a farewell for me as I went off to seminary. My friend William Downey was there. He and I were the same age and grew up in the same church. We had been confirmed together by the same pastor, Pastor Weertz (the father of musician Roger Williams). Bill was more liberal than I. He had attended Grinnell College where he was active in issues of war and peace.

Bill came to see me that last night after lights-out—in my tent at about eleven o'clock. He had come to tell me that he had also made up his mind to be a Lutheran minister. I told him that I was surprised but happy.

He spent a year at Western Seminary in Fremont, Nebraska, a conservative small town. He fit in like a skunk at a garden party. I found out later that I was also supposed to attend that particular seminary. I didn't know it at the

Myself and my mother, Anna Groh Simmons

time, but they (the churches and synods) all had their way of doing business. I was attending Northwestern Seminary in Minneapolis, not an "approved" seminary by the synod. Bill had been forced to attend Western because some kind of agreement had been made. Bill didn't belong there.

When he was in seminary, Bill liked to play around with drinking. He got into trouble as soon as he got there. He contacted me and asked if he could attend Northwestern. I said I doubted it, and I suggested Biblical Seminary in New York. I thought they fit Bill better, but it wasn't what he wanted.

By the end of my first year, I faced my own trouble. I was still struggling over becoming a lawyer, which was my father's desire, or becoming a minister of the Gospel, which my mother wanted. I was taught the Good News of the Gospel for peace and justice, but not how to use it in relation to the violence I witnessed in the world. I was confused as to how to handle the moral issues. When I returned to seminary for my second year, I had made the decision to join the Fellowship of Reconciliation. It is a pacifist organization (Jesus was and is a pacifist) and a peace organization. The only way to peace is through forgiveness and reconciliation.

The Fellowship of Reconciliation was founded in 1914 by a Quaker, a Lutheran, an Englishman, and a German, just after the start of World War I.

The men had participated in an ecumenical conference of Christians trying to prevent the war, a group that was broken up by the start of the war. One year later, the United States founded its own Fellowship of Reconciliation. "The FOR has since become an interfaith and international movement with branches and groups in over 40 countries and on every continent. Today the membership of FOR includes Jews, Christians, Buddhists, Muslims, and people of other faith traditions, as well as those with no formal religious affiliation." The group works for peace through fund-raising, sponsorship of peace-promoting events, and education. The FOR utilizes peaceful methods of protest.

The statement of purpose declared by the organization reads as follows:

> The Fellowship of Reconciliation is composed of women and men who recognize the essential unity of all creation and have joined together to explore the power of love and truth for resolving human conflict. While it has always been vigorous in its opposition to war, the Fellowship has insisted equally that this effort must be based on a commitment to the achieving of a just and peaceful world community, with full dignity and freedom for every human being.

The leadership that founded the Fellowship of Reconciliation came to form other (more widely known) groups such as the American Civil Liberties Union (ACLU), Amnesty International, YMCA, Doctors Without Borders, and Hull House (with Jane Adams). I supported these organizations with whatever influence I had, including financial. I have always tithed. We need to understand the need for justice. FOR makes no discrimination based on color or class or creed, only seeking to meet issues of man's inhumanity to his fellow man. Christians need to be involved in organizations that are nonviolent.

Mary Jane and I married in May of 1941. We married where we met: at St. John's Lutheran Church. We were active in the Luther League together. She supported whatever I was involved with as I began my life of ministry and devotion to the ideas of the Fellowship of Reconciliation. At that time, I had no idea what the future would hold! Mary Jane and I were active in Mr. and Mrs. Groups out of the church and tried to get congregations to have couples involved in community groups bridging gaps in racism. She would become a stabilizing influence—keeping me from going off the road

(I wanted to get involved in every cotton-picking thing, and I wanted to help everyone!). We had three children: John Stewart born in 1944, Virginia Louise born in 1946, and James Stewart born in 1952. Each of my three children was born on a Sunday morning . . . I wonder if God was also trying to tell me to take a break!

My family with Mary Jane

When I was in my third year of seminary, I was already destined to become pastor of St. Mark's Lutheran Church in Minneapolis. I was also president of the board of the Lutheran Hospital Society in Minnesota. The executive of the board was Harold Belgum. Harold's father had been a Lutheran minister in Fargo, North Dakota, where he served three congregations each Sunday.

Harold's brother, David Belgum, had a problem, and he contacted me. He was told by the president of Luther Seminary in St. Paul that he couldn't return for his third year because he didn't believe in literal interpretation of the Bible. I went to work when Harold asked for my help. I told Dr. Paul Roth, president of Northwestern Lutheran Seminary and council member at St. Mark's Lutheran Church where I was pastor, the story. I asked him to let David attend Northwestern Seminary. I made David an associate pastor at St. Mark's so he could fund his stay at Northwestern.

David went on to do some life-changing work for many individuals in the business of counseling. After he was ordained, I helped him take an opportunity at a well-known pastoral counseling place in Boston. He served a Danish parish, enabling him to support himself. He went on to become the director of a clinical pastoral education program and a professor of religious studies at the University of Iowa. He has been published thirty-two times. His areas of specialty include religion and personality, and religion and health.

Bill Downey also contacted me for help around the time of my final year of seminary. He kept telling me he wanted to be ordained with me. Boy, was that a burden on me! I was not in charge of any admissions, but I was a member of the faculty church. I told him I didn't know if I could do anything. I told him to write his own letter and that I would speak to Dr. Roth. I was already youth minister and set to be pastor when I graduated. Dr. Roth agreed.

We went to the same classes and talked all the time. We both went before the examining committee at the same time—the committee in Milwaukee, Wisconsin, which was far more conservative than our synod. Bill got through it fine. My views of biblical literalism, the Virgin Birth, church, and war were divisive and opposed by many in power. World War II had begun. I was already a member of the Fellowship of Reconciliation, considered a pacifist (and antipatriotic) organization. (The Milwaukee crowd was giving birth to the McCarthy crowd!)

I spent nearly three hours before the committee. I had questions about many of the doctrines I was supposed to believe. I finally was approved, though not unanimously, for ordination. According to the story, I made it by one vote, eight to seven! I was seriously ill with a fever of 104 degrees. I was ordained that evening, May 7, 1942, but kept in a room by myself. I was ushered in, ordained, and then taken out right away. I returned to Minneapolis by train and spent the following ten days in Fairview Hospital undergoing treatment for pneumonia. Many of my friends later said of my ordination, "You were out of your mind."

Perhaps my friends were right. My questions of the church doctrine (Lutheran and others) plagued me the rest of my days in the ministry. I was installed pastor of St. Mark's Lutheran in Minneapolis in June of 1942. The congregation first sent me to a camp to help Native Americans and to recuperate from my illness. My friend Bill went to Hope Lutheran Church in South Minneapolis. We saw each other regularly at clergy meetings. About six to eight months into serving that congregation, Bill told me he was going

Ordination Day

into the chaplaincy. I said, "WHAT!" But I told him he had the right to be wrong, and I'd support him as a friend. He joined the navy.

HIS GOSPEL IN MY MINISTRY

Sermon preached at St. Matthew's Lutheran Church in North Hollywood, California, on the fifteenth anniversary of ordination, May 5, 1957. 1 Thessalonians 2:4-12.

Fifteen years in the ministry. So it will be on Tuesday of this week. I have reread the ordination service many times in recent weeks. You see, when I was ordained in 1942, I was "out of my head." I had a fever of 104 from double pneumonia. I can still remember being kept in a side room until the actual moment to kneel with six others for the laying on of the hands. Then out I went to a waiting car, train, and a hospital bed in Minneapolis, Minnesota.

Some of my friends and perhaps most of my enemies believed that I must have been "out of my head" to ever give my life to the Gospel ministry. Perhaps they still do. I had fully intended to enter the profession of law. My entire high school and university career was pointed in that direction. I graduated from Drake University with the same goal in my conscious mind.

As I now review in my mind what happened to me, I know I was restless and uncertain about the choice I had announced and defended against all comers. I was haunted by my unconscious desire to serve God in serving others in a more direct and definite way. I redoubled my efforts to convince myself and others that I wanted to be a lawyer. I know why I did this. I had lost my real desire and direction. All to no avail. God had tapped me on the shoulder. I entered seminary in the fall of 1939. I was ordained May 7, 1942.

The ministry is full of romance. It has its great experiences—warm, tender, profound, loving. It has its heartaches, tears, loneliness, and disappointments. Please don't feel sorry for me or pity me or pin a black crepe medal on me. God's grace has been sufficient for me. He has given my life meaning, purpose, strength, and goal.

I don't mean that the Gospel ministry has been easy for me. Nor has it been an easy way to make a living. Nor has it been an easy way of living— quite the contrary. I find it difficult to live with myself. I am difficult to live with—ask my wife, my family, and my friends. I have been sorely tempted many times to join the mad scramble to make money without the strain and pain of a pastoral life. Few men like to live their life in a goldfish bowl.

I was led in my search for the meaning of His Gospel in my ministry to Paul's letter to the congregation on Thessalonica. He writes for himself and for Silvanus and Timothy, hence the use of the first person plural *we*. I can find no better words to express my understanding of my task in the light of His Gospel. "We speak under the solemn sense of being entrusted by God with the Gospel. We do not aim to please men, but to please God, who knows us thru and thru . . . . Because we loved you, it was a joy to us to give you not only the Gospel of God but our very hearts—so dear did you become to us . . . . Our only object was to help you to live lives worthy of the God who has called you to share the splendor of His Kingdom."

His Gospel has helped me in my ministry by reminding me that He did not choose me to be a pastor to please men, but to please God. Even God can't please some people. Many people get mad at God. He does interfere with living. The most religious people engineered the crucifixion of God's son. People often expect the impossible. Usually they demand more from the pastor than they demand from themselves. People are often petty and small in their attitudes. When they don't get their own way, they get hopping mad.

The most disillusioning experience comes from empty pews, which represent the people whose lives are not worthy of the God who has called them to share in the splendor of His Kingdom. It is an exacting task to preach and teach and witness to the Gospel of God. He is. He lives. He rules. To make this clear in and out of season in a real, vivid, and practical way is a difficult task for me.

Likewise, it is a demanding task to make clear to every man and to all men the Gospel for their lives and for all of their relationships in life. He loves you. He became what you are, to make you what He is. You are worth everything to God. To keep proclaiming in the midst of living contradictions that life to be abundant must be spiritual-centered not thing-centered is not easy. But He calls, gathers, enlightens, and completes everyman's life. I am His witness, His servant. I serve only Him.

The ministry is a task alive with temptation. Pastors are human with their faults and sins. We are not paragons of virtue. We ask ourselves some very disturbing questions. Let me share with you some questions I have asked myself about my ministry. Do I suffer from I-strain with the Big I and the Little God? Am I a perfectionist? Does my tenseness, my inability to relax, my "whole hog or nothing" attitude, my overreaction to criticism and my overanxiety to avoid it, my inhibitions, and my compulsions reveal that I am a perfectionist? Do I suffer from the pride of elation, the pride of being admired, popular? Am I impatient with myself and with other people?

There are more questions which indicate the temptations a pastor faces. In every area of my relationships, these temptations keep reoccurring. In preaching, for instance, I ask myself, is my preaching sharing the insights, understanding, and strength of the Gospel, or merely preaching at people? Am I a mere "peddler" of the Gospel afraid to offend anybody? Am I free from self-display and a desire to have power over people rather than with people? In pastoral relationships, am I afraid to love, or am I afraid of its dangers, and so rigidly oppress that love? Do I believe that loving others is a threat to my pride, an undermining of my dignity, an indication of softness?

His Gospel in the temptations of my ministry has brought me many times to repentance and to acceptance of His forgiveness when I yielded to temptation. God doesn't pamper my prejudices and sins merely because I am His minister. God doesn't coddle me and make me feel cocksure and self-satisfied. He humbles me. He doesn't exempt me from the law of Christian love. He reminds me that He loves me. God doesn't pay any attention to the success-web compulsions of anybody, least of all His ministers. He reminds me that I overwork, that I am overambitious and self-justifying because I am afraid of failure before men. There is no failure before Him except my failure to be faithful in my witness to His saving power.

The ministry of His Gospel is my most rewarding task. This above all I know. I am privileged to help people form their ideals, to stir their consciences, to widen their vision, and to sharpen their concern for others. I see more of real life and living in almost any day than most people see in a year or a lifetime. It is an exciting adventure to serve the creative and significant movements in the community, to express the Gospel in daily life. It is a venture to wage the battle against race and class prejudice and discrimination, to seek justice for all people, to work day in and day out for world peace, to pick up the broken pieces of people's lives and help them find health and wholeness again. It is life's greatest privilege.

CHAPTER TWO

What Am I to Do?

The year 1942 was a big and busy year for me (amid many such years!). I met Hubert H. Humphrey when I was invited to a group called the Young Turks at the University of Minnesota. The Young Turks was a political discussion group comprised of members from the University of Minnesota and Macalester College located in St. Paul. The Young Turks recognized the need for a new liberal party in Minnesota. A whole group of us—including Max Kampelman, Orville Freeman, Arthur Naftalin, and Walter Mondale—began the reorganization of the two liberal parties in Minnesota, the Democratic Party and the Farmer Labor Party.

We would attend meetings of the Farmer Labor Party to garner support. It took a lot of time and effort. We knew all too well that you could never leave a meeting with your opponents still there. They'll undo what you did. Eventually we won enough votes to change the whole Farmer Labor Party, and the rest of the state followed. It took two years to take over the party to complete the merger. In 1944, the Democratic Farmer Labor Party came into being.

Hubert and I became close friends during this process. He thought I had a lot of talent. He got me involved in all kinds of stuff I was interested in doing. I, in turn, had him come to youth groups and conferences. Hubert became the state work progress administrator. He joined a church in Southeast Minneapolis and taught every Sunday morning out at the large Methodist church.

Hubert Horatio Humphrey was an inspiration—a friend and confidante throughout my life. His family—especially his wife, Muriel, and his sons—

also became my friends. He was, to me, the voice and vote for peace and justice between people and the economic and religious opponents of both. From the moment of my going to Northwestern Seminary, my admiration for what he said and the leadership he gave shaped my life and work as a pastor, not only in the "beloved community" but also in the struggles in politics.

Hubert met and married Muriel Buck in the mid-1930s. They moved to Minneapolis. Hubert was educated there then went on to get his master's from Louisiana State University. He wrote his master's thesis on the social teachings of the Bible, especially of Jesus. While in school, Hubert had no intention of running for political office. He returned to Minneapolis, a Republican city with labor union battles.

Hubert made his first run for mayor in the 1943 election, prior to the party merger. I was active in his campaign. He entered sixteen days before the election and raised $12,000 for the race. We didn't expect him to win, but he did take an impressive 47 percent of the vote.

Hubert ran again in the 1945 election to a win. As mayor, he did much to change the landscape of Minnesota. With the chief of police, he broke up the gangster ring and reformed the police force. Minneapolis was known as the anti-Semitism capital. Hubert changed that. He held no prejudice against Jews interested in what we were doing. Many joined his administration.

I kept busy on the human relations reforms he sought in Minneapolis. He formed the Council on Human Relations and rejected the idea of making it a federation of existing groups or of including in its membership professional workers in the human relations field. He also rejected the idea of making it an organization of big names. He appointed eighteen individual citizens who could be expected to garner results. The goal was to assure the opportunity for full and equal participation by all the citizens of Minneapolis in every phase of community life.

Minneapolis became one of the first cities in the country to enact a fair employment law in February 1947 (over a year past the original proposal by Mayor Humphrey). Not everyone was as excited as we were to face the race issues in our community. It took months of organizing a community self-survey on human relations for many to even acknowledge there was a problem serious enough to warrant the adoption of such an ordinance.

Integration of those job fields that demand cross-cultural interactions, those of the police and fire departments, came first. It was the best thing that could have happened. When your job is to protect and to serve, it is not only for upper-class white people. Integration of these public sector jobs enriched police and firemen, helping them become more effective problem solvers, better protectors. The opportunity to communicate with and work with people of other backgrounds helped each worker better understand some of the people and situations encountered in the community.

I should illustrate what Minneapolis was like. There were more Lutherans than people at that time. That should give you an idea of the racial makeup of the city, though it was the attitude of the people that was the problem. The executive secretary of the YMCA (where I worked while at Drake), Arthur Crawford, had at one time introduced me to a young black man named William Chisholm from Rock Hill. William, or Bill, had constructed a building in his hometown where he educated and trained domestics for white people. He was trying to give people a meaningful life.

While I was the pastor of Saint Mark's Lutheran Church in Minneapolis, I got a call from Bill. His building was burned to the ground. The local fire department did little to find the arsonists or to give assistance to rebuild the training institute. I wrote the mayor of Rock Hill and the bank president concerning Bill. The only response I got put Bill as someone with little sense or importance. Bill came north and stayed with my family in the St. Mark's parsonage in Minneapolis. Some of the neighbors were critical. The next-door neighbor was a beer distributor who parked his truck illegally in the backyard. He was never fined. Yet he and other neighbors didn't approve of "niggers" and were clearly unhappy for the duration of Bill's four-day stay.

Bill sang and wrote poetry. After his visit with me, he traveled to speak and sing to raise money to rebuild his burned-down school. He was determined! Here is one of his poems:

What Am I to Do?

If you bar me because I am untidy,
I smile and make myself immaculate,
Returning to be accepted.
If you exclude me because I do not measure up educationally,
I go away and study for a year,
And return happily, assured of welcome.
If you reject me because I am physically unfit,
I take proper treatment to become strong.
If you say that I am not alert, that I am lazy
Or sluggish, I force myself to faster steps
Until they become part of me.

> If you bar me because I am too emotional in my religion
> I let my devotion flow as serene and quiet waters—
> (But never shall I become cold and complacent toward
> My God!)
> With acquiescence shall I strive to please you.
> But if you bar me because of my color alone—
> Then what in this world am I to do?

This poem reflects a great deal what was going on in Minnesota and much of the country at the time. The issue of race was huge. Segregation made all black people out to be second- or third-rate citizens. Civil rights were still being violated, but people were taking a stand. Out of the leadership that started the Fellowship of Reconciliation came the establishment of the American Civil Liberties Union (ACLU), Amnesty International, the YMCA, Hull House, and the Lutheran Peace Fellowship. Participation in these organizations has enriched my coping skills when I witness against injustice. Hubert Humphrey's Commission on Human Relations also did a lot to influence me and the community I was part of.

Even American celebrities faced segregation. When world champion prizefighter Joe Louis came through Minnesota, reservations were made for him at the Radisson Hotel. In his prime, Joe Louis was denied the right to stay on the grounds of his skin color. The six foot two fighter grabbed the Radisson employee by the collar and demanded a room. This singular incident changed Minneapolis. Black people were no longer denied rooms based solely on the color of their skin.

Another famous victim of racism was singer Marian Anderson. Anderson's talent took her around the world, yet she was not permitted to perform in her own nation's capital. Eleanor Roosevelt left the Daughters of the American Revolution in an act of protest, as the concert hall denying Anderson was owned by the group. In support of Anderson, John Cowles Jr., editor of the *Des Moines Register*, allowed her to sing in his home. An outraged Eleanor Roosevelt arranged for Marian Anderson to perform for FDR and Queen Elizabeth at a private concert in the White House.

A national group that I was part of locally in Minneapolis is called the Urban League. The mission of this organization is to help African Americans with issues pertaining to economic independence, equality, and civil rights. As a member of the Urban League, I participated in activities meant to help African Americans become part of the community both recreationally and economically. One activity was to reserve lanes at the local bowling alley that normally excluded African Americans. We would then bring a group of black people in to bowl on our reserved lanes. Since restaurants would do things such as salt dishes ordered by black people so much that no human could eat it, members of the UL, including myself, would often order meals then turn them over to an African American.

Our most memorable project was the desegregation of department stores in Minneapolis. Dayton's was the largest most influential chain there. Donald Dayton himself was a Presbyterian, and it seems we were able to appeal to his sense of God's love for all. With the attention of the Fair Employment Practice Commission, Donald Dayton contacted the UL. He agreed to employ a black man after we'd gathered enough signatures from customers agreeing to be served by anyone, regardless of race, who was competent. We got the signatures, and Donald Dayton hired an African American from Philadelphia in the luggage department.

A challenge arose when other employees refused to work with that (or any) black man. Fortunately when Mr. Dayton began firing anyone who refused to work with his new employee, most of the men changed their minds.

Other stores would soon follow suit. The Urban League had begun the process of desegregation of department stores in Minneapolis. Victory is not an end. In fact, it's usually another beginning. There was still a long road ahead. Black people were only allowed positions in the sales department. We wanted more. There was still hope that we could change opportunities in the office and clerical fields. If you can't make it work where you are (seize the opportunity locally), you can't make it work nationally. We helped set a precedent for the National Urban League, and we changed the racial landscape of one very white city. We improved the lives of some by getting others to look past their hate using creativity and love.

Not everyone was eager to accept this change as necessary. The work we had done was a start and an example. Civil rights issues have not disappeared in Minnesota or any place else. Recent legislation in the United States allocating funds to solve old civil rights cases is an indication that civil rights violations are still issues. That doesn't mean that incidents have stopped. Not all old civil rights cases are cold cases.

I participated in civil rights work and preached about it to my congregation. I was often criticized. When I preached to the congregation or synod on a moral issue, I often heard that that was not my responsibility. As a member of the Fellowship of Reconciliation, I was still plagued by questions. The kind of preaching I believe in changes the focus of laws. You must connect your preaching with your acts.

Humphrey's win was a high as I experienced some exciting years and events. A low also came during this time, in 1945. It is very painful, shocking. I was preaching in Des Moines when I found out about the first bomb (Ike later said it was unnecessary!). Hiroshima. My old friend Bill Downey was the chaplain in the South Pacific on the Enola Gay—the B-29 bomber that dropped the atomic bomb on Hiroshima. He gave the prayer blessing the dropping of the bomb. They killed one hundred thousand people. This was not a Christian prayer. Leading Protestant theologian Reinhold Niebuhr called it the worst prayer of the century. I couldn't have lived with myself if it were me.

Jesus opposed war and the violence that fuels it. For over sixty years as an ordained Lutheran pastor, I have opposed six major wars—World War II, Korean War, Vietnam War, Operation Desert Storm, Iraq, and the war going on in Afghanistan and Pakistan. War with violence is sinful and wrong. God's answer is forgiveness and reconciliation in love. The Fellowship of Reconciliation affirms nonviolence in love, following Jesus's way of love—enemies and friends in every relationship in life is the Gospel, the good news of God. Reconciliation is a much more difficult task than any other way (Jesus paid the price of crucifixion, and you don't get off the hook easily either).

When Bill returned, we maintained our friendship. Bill knew how I felt about war and prayer. He took a church in Foxpoint, Wisconsin, a wealthy suburb of Milwaukee, and became extremely right wing. His personal habit of drinking became worse. He couldn't live within himself. He became zealous about punishing people who did not believe as he did. My question is: What did he do in that parish to get support for such a tragedy?

The answer to that, unfortunately, is likely not much. Bill Downey served a congregation made up of leadership involved in war. VIOLENCE IS THE NUMBER ONE PROBLEM THE WORLD FACES. People get involved with violence because of war. War is a result of "me-ism," and the resulting "isms"—racism, sexism, classism, and poverty. John 3:16 is used to justify the killing of Jesus. Christianity centers on the belief that Jesus was sent by God to die so that "we" sinful humans could be reconciled by God. Bill Downey and other "believers" like him become "enforcers," enforcing who was saved based on those personal "me-isms."

I have had a lovers' quarrel with the church. I'm hung up on the refusal of the church to address the problem of violence as a solution. How could the original Gospel of love be used to justify the torture, conquest, and bloodletting carried out by devout Christians against others? I love the church, but my disagreements have come from my belief in the Jesus message of nonviolent love, seeking justice, and peace for all people. We have trivialized the Gospel of Jesus's nonviolent love, comforting the afflicted but not afflicting the comfortable.

In 1948, I made the decision to leave the congregation I served, St. Marks, to run for political office. I didn't run as a clergyman. I wanted people to consider me for me. My beliefs as a Christian definitely shaped my politics, but I was not seeking political office to convert the masses to Lutheranism. I wanted to make sweeping changes to the social makeup of Minneapolis. I sought justice and equality, and renounced violence. The conservatives made it clear they still didn't believe there was a human relations problem in our town. Republican opinion was, "We don't want another Hubert Humphrey on our hands."

Support from Hubert Humphrey during
my run for mayor of Minneapolis

Hubert, as mayor of Minneapolis, had already begun establishing himself as a leader of civil rights. At the 1948 Democratic National Convention he wrote a minority plank for non-segregation that was voted as the majority plank, arguing with these unforgettable words, "To those who say, my friends, to those who say, that we are rushing this issue of civil rights, I say to them we are 172 years too late! To those who say, this civil rights program is an infringement on states' rights, I say this: the time has arrived in America for the Democratic Party to get out of the shadow of states' rights and walk forthrightly into the bright sunshine of human rights!" (At that moment the Dixiecrat party formed and nominated Strom Thurman. They felt deserted by their own candidate, Harry Truman, and hoped to take votes away from him.)

I believe that my support of fair employment cost me the mayoral election in 1949. By then, Humphrey had been elected to the senate, and I faced acting mayor Eric Hoyer. I was glad for the work Hubert Humphrey and I had done to change the party divisions in Minneapolis seven years earlier. The church had been supportive of my decision though I had officially resigned at the beginning of the election year.

I needed the continued support! My run for mayor left me jobless and in debt. I spent time doing "odd jobs." I helped found the Minnesota Fund, a mutual fund, and became part of the sales staff selling shares. I wrote financial how-to articles. I also became involved with a radio station doing two news programs. One was called *Inside the News*, with a tagline "for people on the outside." The other was called *Food for Thought*.

A short career in radio

In 1951, Mary Jane and I moved to North Hollywood, California. I had accepted a call from St. Matthew's Lutheran Church. There was pressure to run for mayor there, but I decided to stay in the ministry (for the time being!). I joined the North Hollywood YMCA board. A member of St. Matthew's had lived next door to Adlai Stevenson in Illinois. When Stevenson came to town, I got to talk to him. I worked on the campaign for his election.

CHAPTER THREE

Lovers' Quarrel

We live in a world in which the primary emphasis among Christians, at least in this country, is to come and accept Jesus as your Lord and savior, and to get all of the members of your family to accept that same formula. When the Church is known by "for me, it requires of me only that I help it grow, get more members," that is not the Gospel. The Gospel is not loyalty to our flag and our military. I've had enough of the Billy Grahams, Jerry Falwells, Pat Robertsons, and those "God is on our side, God is on my side, our chosen enemies are God's enemies and I'll put up my defenses" attitudes. But violence only provokes more violence.

Jack Nelson-Pallmeyer contends, "Without roots in the nonviolent character of God, Jesus will be dismissed as an interim ethic . . . linked to Jesus as a 'Paschal Lamb' slaughtered to be God as part of an interred ethic—No longer relevant." Jesus disappeared when he was named the one God sent to die for my sins. Jesus's message of nonviolent love was literally displaced. I DO NOT BELIEVE THAT JESUS WAS SENT BY GOD TO DIE FOR MY SINS—HE DIED BECAUSE HE LIVED A LIFE OF NONVIOLENT LOVE.

Pallmeyer makes clear that the Eucharist meal makes God a bloodthirsty, punishing deity, using Jesus's blood sacrifice to avoid the violent judgment of God. God turns out then not to be a loving God but rather to be something that could be used as a dominating power. This violent God is a preposterous idea—what kind of God would send someone to do *that* to you? We cannot worship a God who punishes. He is a loving God. God's grace is a free gift (and Jesus is not the rescuer).

Religion is a problem in society. Catholicism and Protestantism engage in domination using God and the Bible to dehumanize. Religion and scripture are used in such a way that oppresses women (and oppresses gays and lesbians, and tolerates segregation). Rabbi Abraham Heschel said, "Racism is the greatest threat to humanity—the maximum amount of hatred for the minimum of reason—the maximum of cruelty for the minimum of thinking."

Martin Luther believed this single most important thing: nobody is saved except by God's grace. What is in a person's past that demonstrates that person's worthiness or unworthiness for a penalty or a benefit? Grace asks what a person needs. Grace is a gift. You don't need to pay for it by a man-imposed, devised way. When Luther protested the sale of indulgences, he had no intention of leaving the Catholic Church—they threw him out. He was excommunicated as a heretic, and there was a bounty on his head. When ecclesiasts decide the truth and punish everyone who steps off the line, it is domination, and the basis of heresy.

When I was pastor of St. Mark's, a young man named George Crist came to me. George Crist was a graduate of Carthage and wanted to attend Northwestern Seminary. His problem was that he had no job and no money. I hired him to do half-time youth work and half-time cleaning at St. Mark's for a salary. George easily became a part of the church community. He fell in love with and married the church secretary, Evelyn Schultz.

George Crist graduated from Northwestern and went to Bethlehem Lutheran Church in Durham, Wisconsin. That was during the time I left Minnesota for California. In 1955 when I was sponsored by the British Council of Churches to go to Europe, I picked up a copy of the *New York Times* in the airport. Bold headlines announced that my friend Reverend George Crist was on trial for heresy. My old friend Reverend William Downey played a part behind the scenes. He was not on the committee, but he helped to make sure George was tried for heresy. He believed people like Crist who don't believe in the doctrine of the Virgin Mary shouldn't be in the ministry.

Though death is no longer a consequence, heresy trials embody the violence and injustice of the crusades. George Crist was found guilty and was defrocked, as they say, or removed from the Lutheran Church. He took a Unitarian church for a while. George's beliefs were not heretical. They allowed him to serve another congregation with a different set of beliefs.

In the history of the church during the first three centuries, there were relatively small communities of people trying to live Jesus's way of life. These groups first consisted of Jews and Gentiles. They sold all their property so all groups had an even amount of resources. There were no soldiers. There weren't cathedrals. Worship was in home chapels. People came, enjoyed the fellowship and the Word, and began the service of deeds. There were no needs.

As the group grew, Constantine looked for something to make the group "absolute." In AD 325, he declared Christianity the official religion of the empire. The papacy and the hierarchy of the cardinals were given the task to decide the creeds, the confessions, the doctrines (the Apostles' Creed, Nicene Creed, Athanasian Creed, and Augsburg Confession do not save). The rules were made and enforced, and those who disobeyed were punished, including trial and punishment for heresy. They made converts by force if necessary. And so for four hundred-plus years, we had **the Crusades** with violence as an approved method of conversion.

The crusades are a black mark on the church of Jesus Christ. They deny the Gospel of Jesus's message. He lived the message and was crucified by the Romans as a threat to the Roman Empire. His message of love without violence was ignored. The word *crusade* always reminds me of the four centuries when the "saved" made war against the "heathens." I find it bothersome that Billy Graham used the term *crusade* when referring to his form of evangelism. The crusades consisted of centuries of murder. Thousands who did not believe were killed.

My first encounter with Billy Graham was in 1947. He came to Minnesota to meet with the Head of the World Fundamentalists at a Baptist Church in Minneapolis. Simultaneously there was a meeting of the National Council of Churches. I was president of the Protestant Ministerial Association. Dr. E. Stanley Jones was scheduled to speak to our group. Billy Graham didn't like the simultaneous meeting and took issue that Jones was not born-again. Graham and I then went back and forth a while via the local Minneapolis press. Our encounter began a lifelong challenge to the Billy Graham idea of salvation.

Billy Graham traveled the country holding huge events where people would come forward claiming they'd suddenly found the Lord—rallies to gain converts. He called them "crusades." I visited one such "crusade." A young man who answered the altar call and was saved returned to his seat next to me, looking bug-eyed. He asked, "Are you saved?" I looked him straight on and asked, "From what? To what? For what?"

Graham received a boost in popularity when William Randolph Hearst told his chain of newspapers to give Billy Graham support as the savior of the USA. The instruction Hearst gave to his staff was "puff Graham." That was a real boost to Graham who had an obsessive need for approval by the rich and powerful. He was popularized and used his notoriety as his way of getting people into the church. Graham has been the unofficial chaplain to the White House (often inviting himself) from Eisenhower to the most recent president Bush (with Carter and Clinton as exceptions).

I followed Billy Graham for his whole ministry. Billy Graham's Gospel is a half-Gospel, the wrong half! Accept Jesus Christ as your personal Lord and savior and you get a pass into heaven and escape from hell. Theologian Reinhold Niebuhr says that the success of mass evangelism "depends on oversimplifying every issue." Sins such as lying, swearing, and drinking occupy sermons (rather than the subject of injustice). Billy Graham and others like him have made Christianity into nothing but a selfish "get saved" document. He never insisted on a Gospel of peace and justice.

First, there are no individual Christians. God hasn't made a deal with you that God hasn't offered everybody. But what does the Lord require of me? We live in a world of individualism and me-ism. We evaluate everything we do by whether it is good for me. Me-ism is a disease. Greed is our mantra. We evaluate our relationship to our church congregation on the same basis. What do I get out of this relationship? What does it require of me?

Billy Graham's ministry ignores the difficult aspects of Christian life. We are many diverse communities in our world, each with our own history. We have many races, religions, and ways of living. These differences have often resulted in violence to dominate another community and take their resources as ours. We need to live in relationship to people—not to institutions. You may belong to an institution, but your relation is to the people. We belong to each other.

Institutions are responsible for degrading ideas—racism, sexism, classism, etc. Jesus was a Jew. Jesus observed every Jewish holiday. He spoke often as from that group. Then anti-Semitism became accepted (or desired) under the guise of the creeds. Domination led to centuries of anti-Semitism even though the majority of people involved with the early church were Jewish.

People I've met and worked with were not all Christians or Jews or any other religion. I worked with nonreligious people as well as with unbelievers. My relationship to other faiths is not a theological one, but a moral one. In Minneapolis, where Lutherans outnumbered people, I was chosen by the Minnesota Jewish Council to be a spokesman for them. An attorney friend of mine, Barry Weiss, had this to share about me speaking of shortly after we met in 1965:

> John came to our house to deliver some legal papers to me. He was dressed in his clergy garb. [My wife] Sande, her mother, and our then 8 month old son, Steven, were there. Now, you have to understand that in 1965 Jewish people were pretty suspicious of Christian clergy people, as active anti-Semitism in the US was still alive in some quarters and a good deal of it came from churches, at least in our view. John immediately got on the floor and started crawling with Steven, charming him. He then spoke to Sande's mother at length in such a compassionate way that I believe my mother in law in that moment revised her whole attitude about Christian clergy!

Religions have denominations in abundance, about thirty-eight thousand Christian denominations in the world today. Mark Twain, in "The Lowest Animal," said, "[Man] is the only animal that has the True Religion—several of them." Whose doctrine is right? Which religion is true? Who gets to decide? Not you and not me. Jesus confronted, condemned, and challenged the political and religious powers that dominated people's lives, ALL people's lives.

Nearly everyone who signed the Constitution believed in God. They believed that religion promoted individual morality and civic virtue. They didn't want the national government to meddle in affairs of religion or conscience with an established particular religion or church. James Madison had seen ministers of the Gospel imprisoned because they weren't of the so-called right faith. He was passionate in his own faith, but more passionate about protecting the faith of other people. James Madison and Thomas Jefferson insisted that forcing conformity to a particular faith, doctrine, or polity by governmental law would make people "either hypocrites or fools."

I am a member of Americans United for the Separation of Church and State. We are considered an irritant to Billy Graham and the evangelists. They use and misuse the First Amendment, the Second Amendment, and the Fifth Amendment. The separation of church and state is fundamental, though grossly misunderstood and misused.

The presence of someone like Billy Graham in the White House is a threat to democracy. The United States has been on a slow drift toward a theocracy. In 1954, "under God" was added to the Pledge of Allegiance (signed by President Eisenhower after Senator Joe McCarthy called Eisenhower a "dedicated Communist"). In 2002, President Bush said he would only propose judicial nominees who "believe our rights come from God." In 2004, the Internal Revenue Service had to crack down on churches and their leaders politicking, violating the law that forbids churches to aid candidates for public office. We also need notice that Franklin Graham, Billy Graham's son, heads Samaritan's Purse, a charity questioned for its receipt of federal funds under allegations (in more countries than our one) of proselytization.

The oath of the president does not include "so help me God." "In God we Trust" did not always appear on our currency. It only became our national motto when McCarthyism created the hysteria that godless Communism was getting control of the United States. The original motto chosen by John Adams, Benjamin Franklin, and Thomas Jefferson—E Pluribus Unum (Of Many, One)—celebrates plurality, not theocracy.

There are Christian Nationalists within the dominating groups in this country. Christian Nationalism is not a Christian movement. It is a nationalistic political movement that cloaks itself in religion. The Roman Catholic Church still dominates the Christian world and makes up a large number of Christian Nationalists. I've read that people not baptized according to the formula (anything not according to the Trinity) had to be rebaptized. It's oppressive. Recent sex scandals in the Catholic Church were all over the news for a while. It becomes oppressive when it spends time denying it. When the church settled pedophilia charges out of court, it protected the control of the hierarchy.

Often misunderstood is that the separation of religion from life is pure heresy. It contradicts the biblical witness and understanding of my faith. It makes worship in all its forms the ONLY function of the church. Jesus was a theologian as well as an acute observer of the political scene. He understood how theology and politics needed to be seen in relation to each other. He was crucified as a political criminal.

In a sermon titled "The Odd Couple," I discussed the so-called divorce between religion and politics. The scriptures are full of illustrations of the relationship between man and God, of man's attitude toward God, and of man's relationship with God and his fellow man in the life of economics, politics, and social living. Moses protested the Pharaoh on economics, politics, and the social order (in the name of God). Politics and religion have always been inseparable.

The problem with Billy Graham's role in the White House is this—he never spoke truth to power. Richard Nixon used Billy Graham, and Billy still never confronted Nixon about Watergate. Graham also got in hot water with Nixon over a discussion of the "total Jewish domination of the media." Graham denied saying anything about left-wing Jews dominating with "a stranglehold that has got to be broken or the country's going down the drain," but a 1972 Oval Office recording captured his words. Graham later apologized, and he wrote and preached against racial prejudice.

Billy's sermon in the National Cathedral after 9/11 was disgraceful. Graham said that many of the victims were now in heaven and would not want to come back because it's so glorious and wonderful. Nothing about 9/11 was wonderful. A critic wrote, "We should not have to choose between being imbeciles and being mourners." It is not consoling. It is insulting. We are not a country of children.

Billy Graham's son blamed New Orleans for Hurricane Katrina. He blamed the city and residents "for engaging in satanic worship" and "social perversion." He said, "God is going to use that storm to bring revival." All religions and all denominations have been dominated by political and church political power. It has already been decided what is to be believed, who is to teach it, and how it is to be enforced. We are called a Christian Nation. We are not.

In 1955, I attended the international convention of YMCA in Paris, France. I traveled to Germany, Italy, and Switzerland. I was also chosen one of the top ten preachers by the British Council of Churches. It was a sort of pulpit exchange. Mary Jane came along for two months in Scotland and England.

In 1955, Billy Graham was also in Europe, in Glasgow, Scotland, for his "tell it on the hearth"-themed crusade. He produced a film to send to America to get people to follow his movement. Graham painted the Scottish Church as decadent and rather un-Christian, then portrayed that he turned the Scottish Church around. The film was rejected by the commission, deciding if the film would carry the approval of the Scottish Church. They said it was defamatory and returned it to the Graham organization to make changes.

The second proposed script was rejected as worse than the first. I was in Scotland two weeks after Graham. The minister who was supposed to bless the script confronted me to view the film. I said thumbs-down to two different scripts. The commissioner then went to London to see Billy Graham in person at his very high-class hotel, with no success. The second version was shown in the USA against the will of the Scottish Church.

We know that in Rome there was no separation between religion and politics. The temple was an institution of enormous political, economic, and religious consequences. The high priest was a political appointee of the Roman Empire. The key players were arrogant, powerful, and cruel because oppression was a systematic necessity. What about now? Anyone promoting religion the way Billy Graham has is no better (and hardly different).

Over the years, the Bible has been used to support salvation by the creeds when that is not the truth. Using the Bible that way is wrong. The church was founded as a domination tool, a control mechanism, an empire, not a democracy. The ecclesiastical structure was exactly like a corporation. There is no basis for that in the scriptures. Bishop John Shelby Spong, an Episcopal, says you are not to be involved with a structure (like that of Graham's, Falwell's, and Roberson's) but rather that you are to be critical of scripture.

Bishop Spong, whose writing has done a number of things for me, looks at what scripture is about and why it is not definitive. He has done an excellent job putting the books of the Bible in their context. The Bible is theology. It is faith seeking understanding. It rejects literalism because literalism ignores the context, the culture, the truth. A lot of things that go into scripture are just not true. The Gospels are not memoirs. Matthew was written late in the first century. There was no hard evidence. Fragments of the Bible have been taken out of context and used as argument. It has been redated to fit. This is socialized myth making!

If you are able to believe in the Bible as the literal Word of God, I ask you: which of the two creation stories do you believe in? The six days of creation are different in the first two chapters of the Bible. Why should women be considered property? Why is it that only men can get a divorce? Furthermore, what do you do when someone in the Old Testament is ordered to kill a family member? Deuteronomy 21:20-21 gives these instructions to parents with a disobedient child: "They shall say to the elders of his town, 'This son of ours is stubborn and rebellious. He will not obey us. He is a glutton and a drunkard.' Then all the men of the town shall stone him to death."

We rebel against accepting myths, but we do it all the time. A right, reasonable person cannot accept the Bible to be the "Word of God." It's a collection of how people viewed things that happened. Spong reminds us that the study of scriptures by competent scholars say a lot of scripture is not true at all. Stories were put in the Bible to serve a purpose. Biblical research has made clear that the specific content of the Bible is centuries old and not valid.

We must keep Jesus of history at the heart of all Christian faith. Jesus focused most of his life and ministry on the domination system as the opposite of God's domination-free, compassion-filled order. He was disinterested in the theme of repentance as a means to avoid God's punishing violence. Jesus exposed the absurd notion that there was only one way to think, one true religion. He called his people to live a different way.

Jesus abandoned morality. The meaning of Christian ethics is not of principle—it is of relationship. People were more important than the rules. He socialized with prostitutes and healed those deemed unclean by the oppressors. Jesus told parables to expose systems of abusive power. His crucifixion was his ultimate identification with those on the wrong side of the moral divide. The Romans called a crucifixion "a slave's punishment." Slaves were the lowest.

Who killed Jesus? Mark, Luke, and John were not witnesses. Jesus was not killed as an atoning sacrifice but as a consequence of his life and faith that conflicted sharply with the ideas of control by Rome and the Temple. Jesus is crucified according to the creeds, under Pontius Pilate, not by Pontius Pilate. Jesus was crucified during the reign of Pontius Pilate who ruled from 26 to 36 CE. The Christian creeds are problematic. Creeds reinforce distortions and downplay the oppressive role played by Roman rulers, treating Jesus as a missing person and exonerating Rome.

Jesus taught that people are more important than the rules. In Rome (and since then with those like Billy Graham), the rules are more important than the people. Morality, then, becomes the key issue. Grace is the opposite of morality. Morality has helped those in power of starving in the midst of plenty. We help only those in need if we determine the person is worthy of our aid. We have abandoned morality out of concern for behavior and called it morality. Morality's function becomes, then, a line drawn between good and bad.

I attended the national convention of the Lutheran Church of America (LCA) in 1955. In 1954, the Supreme Court ruled in favor of Brown who had a case against the board of education. At the '55 convention, I led the movement and debate for the church to confirm the court decision to be a moral decision. **All political decisions are moral demands for behavior on us.** It is important for the church to stand up for moral decisions. This leads to important change. The church and its representatives need to be agents of change.

Rev. John Simmons

Excerpt from "I Ran for Mayor"
From *Campus Lutheran*

Five years ago, I resigned from my parish, St. Mark's Lutheran in Minneapolis, and filed for the office of mayor. I spent six months in active campaigning. My volunteer committee spent nearly $18,000 on the campaign. I, personally, exhausted every cent of savings I had and borrowed some that I spent two years repaying. I won the primary, outdistancing all twelve opponents. I lost the general election six weeks later. I lost but I won.

I won a battle with myself, and I believe I am more effective in my ministry for having had this experience. Reflecting now upon it, I can truly appreciate the public servants that we have who are of high ideals. On the other hand I am concerned for the Christian citizenry, who take so lightly their responsibility.

Where Were the Christians?

Here I must, with pain, report that the overwhelming amount of financial support did *not* come from the active, practicing, professing Christians in the community. The reason may be, in charity, that they aren't concerned enough to know what it costs, they leave it to someone else, or they are supporting your opponent because they don't believe you ought to run for political office. But I believe that eventually we are going to have to support from public funds the campaigns of the two candidates who emerge on top from the primary election, and maybe work out a way to support all candidates from public funds. This would permit a careful check on expenditures and a limitation on them.

The farther away I am from this experience, the more convinced I am of the fact that our campaigns are too long. And they are too hectic. There is no time to reflect upon the split-second decisions you as a candidate must make. You must answer the question now, or you are covering up, dodging, or indulging in generalities, which in honesty of purpose you ought not to do.

The editor of *CAMPUS LUTHERAN* suggested that I not only briefly cover my experience "recollected in tranquility," but that I share with you some general convictions on the responsibility of Christians in the political sphere. I am happy to oblige, conscious as I am that, here, disagreement begins for many Christians.

There is one fact that has burned itself indelibly on my mind. It is unfortunately true. This is that *the chief moral decisions and ultimate loyalties of Christians are determined by the political, economic, and social groups to which they belong, and not by their Christian faith, life, or church.* The great majority of Christians in the area of politics do not think of the ethical teachings of the Gospel. The implications of a love for God and a love for others seem of fringe importance, not relevant and rarely considered in the arena of politics. We avoid coming to grips with these "mundane" issues.

We never fight any particular evil, except the safe ones—liquor, gambling, and prostitution. We advocate brotherhood toward all men, but never specifically as it relates to housing, health, or employment for Negroes or other minorities. We talk of justice, but we never hazard an opinion on what justice may mean in an industrial dispute in our own community. I raise the sixty-four-dollar question: how can you make a moral contribution as a Christian if you refuse to make a decision on any living relevant issue?

Sixty-Four-Dollar Question

I believe that it is *immoral* to refuse to come to grips with specific issues in the light of the principles that are inherent in the Christian Gospel. I believe it is a denial of the Gospel to take refuge in ritualistic trappings, theological speculation, or dogmatism; to fancy oneself as a part of the "saving remnant"; to seek only a well-oiled institution or a hierarchal appendage to the current stream of life; to seek only to improve one's character in isolation. John Dewey (if I may mention his name) put it succinctly: "While the saints are engaged in introspection, burly sinners run the world."

I have discovered that just as some Lutherans are Lutherans first, and Christians second, so likewise Christians are first Republicans or Democrats and secondarily Christians. I remember from my campaign two prominent Christian leaders with whom I had worked in the Church Federation who told me they couldn't support me because I was of the wrong political party. The mayor's position in Minneapolis is a nonpartisan office, and as a matter of fact, in that general election, both candidates were of the same party. Yet these men chose my opponent (who was not identified with any church) because their party was afraid that, in time, I would become a threat to one of their leaders at a higher level of government. And this continually happens to political candidates, regardless of their party.

The point is not to be missed: our first loyalty and the major influence in our decisions in the arena of politics is to the political, economic, or social power group to which we belong, and not to the meaning of the Christian Gospel in its ethical imperatives in the practical situations of life.

Political authority rests on a moral base at all times and in all places. Even the actions of pressure groups and the public cannot escape the measurement of moral standards. This morality is not merely a negative prohibition against evil, but a positive demand for good will and action "in the interests of the universal neighborhood of mankind." Yet we as Protestants have virtually abdicated responsibility for the character of American life. That responsibility we must once more assume.

It is sad to read the public opinion polls of negative attitude the parents of this generation have toward their sons entering politics. This indicates an unhealthy attitude toward democracy itself. Democracy provides the best government for the free expression and growth of Christianity and for its preservation and extension, we need Christian men and women to give leadership. This leadership is needed at all levels of government.

CHAPTER FOUR

Redemption Undeterred

In a Midwest farm area, a farmer and his wife and their only child, a five-year-old daughter lived their lives, ignoring, by choice, their neighbors. All efforts to get them to join with others in the community failed. At dusk one evening when the farmer came to the house, he discovered that his daughter was missing. Frantically he and his wife searched the farm as the darkness closed in on them. Finally the wife ran to the next farm to ask for help.

As the night wore on, nearly fifty people came searching for the little girl. The leader of the group finally suggested that all of them join hands to make a systematic search. They joined hands, and in about half an hour, one of them came upon the body of the little girl facedown in a shallow swamp. The father picked up the lifeless body of his daughter as his newfound friends wept unashamedly. The father cried out, "Why didn't we join hands sooner!"

I shared this story as part of my installation address as Pacoima Memorial Lutheran Hospital administrator in 1962, asking all those present to join hands that the hospital may be part a healing community. Pacoima Memorial Lutheran Hospital was a great triumph, the result of so many holding hands after a tragic situation.

This is among the answers to the question, what's it all about, John?

On January 31, 1957, a fighter jet and a transport aircraft collided over Pacoima Junior High School in Pacoima, California. In those days, boys' recess was different than girls' recess. Two hundred twenty children were on the playground. Five men in the planes died as did three boys on the school playground—Ronnie Brann, Robert Zallan, and Evan Elsner. Seventy-four other children suffered burns, broken bones, and other internal injuries. Victims were rushed all over Los Angeles because the nearest hospital was too small.

I was in North Hollywood, pastor of St. Matthew's Lutheran Church. I was working with another pastor on the start of a new Lutheran church in Pacoima. He and I spent the day seeing that the injured were tended to. I already knew a lot of people in the community. On this day, I met even more. Later I was with Pastor Broadus, a Baptist, at his church. I had worked with him on projects in the San Fernando Valley. The discussion focused on Pacoima, the only city with a population of sixty-one thousand without its own hospital. Out of that discussion formed the decision to raise money for a hospital.

Reverend Hillary Broadus and Marsha Hunt

Here is the problem as outlined by a brochure used to raise money for the hospital:

> The California Department of Public Health and the State Bureau of Hospitals have declared that Pacoima is the only city in the United States having a population of more than 61,000 which does not have its own Class A hospital.

> These agencies have further determined that this part of the San Fernando Valley—including Pacoima, San Fernando, Sylmar,

Granada Hills, Sepulveda, Newhall, Saugus, and all intervening county areas, is in desperate need of hospital facilities. The population of this area is estimated at 131,300. There are now 64 acceptable hospital beds to serve this population. To meet minimum state standards of hospital requirements, 369 additional beds are needed in the area.

Where will our sick and injured go? Where will they find beds? Those who cannot get into the already overcrowded smaller hospitals may end up some 20 miles away, in Los Angeles. In many instances the time required to reach an available bed may mean the difference between life and death.

The need is evident. It is more than evident—it is glaring. And upon us it reflects a responsibility to provide beds to meet the need. We must recognize this responsibility, and together we must act to meet our common need.

There are four ways we face the world. First, some take the world as they find it and make no attempt to change and improve its conditions. Secondly, there are those who try to escape the world. They refuse to admit to reality. Thirdly, there are those who try to change the world to fit their own selfish interests. Last are those who seek to transform the world.

People often think their total responsibility is to give temporary aid—charity, not justice. The crash was uncontrollable. You cannot control events, but you can control your reactions. You can be more than charitable, but it is challenging. We labor under the illusion that we must never accept trouble as part and parcel of life. Jesus did the best things in the worst of times. He creatively and redemptively created, out of trouble, relationships that are helpful and healthy.

Pastor Broadus headed a group to raise money in the community. We sought a government grant so that two-thirds of the money (matching funds guaranteed by the Hill-Burton Act) came from the state and federal governments. Locally we had to come up with the balance. We tapped the industries in Pacoima. The airport had a good leader who pledged a good deal of money.

On December 9, 1957, I was preaching at the ninetieth birthday of a church in Sacramento. After preaching, a group of us, including attorney Ben O'Brien, submitted money to the proper authorities requesting matching funds for the hospital. We had to drive from Sacramento to Berkeley to the Bureau of Hospitals for a ten o'clock appointment. We were told we lacked sufficient money, which meant the whole deal was off.

I suggested we get two hotel rooms and try to raise the money by five o'clock. Everyone thought I was nuts! We spent the day on the phone with folks in Southern California. We had to get people to pledge amounts AND call banks to have their funds verified. We raised about $300,000 by two o'clock. We were set for a meeting at four thirty. The head of the Bureau of Hospitals verified we had enough money. He approved. I almost fainted.

That night I was expected to teach a class for UCLA at eight o'clock at St. Matthew's in North Hollywood. The chief of the Bureau of Hospitals, John Berry, booked a flight for 6:00 p.m. from Oakland to Burbank. I met with nine students at eight. I taught for one and a half hours on foreign policy. I woke the next morning and felt the weight of the task ahead of us!

It is a thrilling experience to be an eyewitness to some great event. It tingles the senses, swells the pride, and is a ready conversation piece. We are witnesses *to* something, not *for* something. We avoid being responsible participants. When we embrace suffering (or tragedy or discovery), we make suffering a creative force in our lives. Suffering teaches, educates, and inspires people with courage. Martin Luther King Jr. said, "To suffer in a righteous cause is to grow to our full stature as a person."

Since the opening of Pacoima Memorial Lutheran Hospital until 1962, I was part-time administrator of the hospital. The synod eventually called me to special service. I accepted and was set to resign from St. Matthew's Lutheran Church to become full-time hospital administrator. My installation was February 18.

February 1, 1962, I was invited to speak by the business and professional chapter of the American Jewish Congress. Actress Marsha Hunt and a Unitarian minister, Reverend Brooks Walker, were also invited to speak. We all met for lunch prior to the event to discuss the topic "The Extreme Right—Threat to Democracy?" The background of this meeting was the overabundance of extremist groups from the Left and the Right in Los Angeles. The evening turned into an example of the severity of the situation. Below is the best recap of the evening provided by Haskell Lazere, coordinator of the event:

> Reverend John G. Simmons had talked to the audience at the Temple about the leaders of the Extreme Right—who they were and what their backgrounds were. He had also defended the right of Extremist groups to expound their ideas in public. Reverend Brooks R. Walker followed Mr. Simmons, repeating the defense of freedom of expression, and going on to compare the methods and objectives of the Extreme Right to those of the Extreme Left.
>
> Marsha Hunt again defended the freedom of the Extreme Right to express their views. Then she spoke about the United Nations, and the specious attacks made on it by Communists as well as the Extreme Right. One by one she tackled the charges and one by one she demolished them. Miss Hunt also noted and criticized the prophets of violence who were preaching the doctrine of a "preventive war" to maintain peace.

Just as [Marsha] Hunt was answering the first question following the presentations, an urgent message was handed up to Reverend Walker asking that he make a telephone call at once. Mr. Walker left the platform immediately, returning in a space of minutes, ashen-faced. He strode to the podium and spoke softly into the microphone. "Excuse me Marsha, but when you spoke earlier about violence, you didn't know how right you were. I've just been informed my house was bombed and I have to leave. My wife and children are safe."

The audience gasped in horror. Reverend Simmons said, "My God, I wonder if they've bombed my home?" and dashed from the platform to call his wife. Marsha Hunt murmured, "We'd all better go home." The meeting was ended, and some milled helplessly about.

It was the most frightening experience for my family. The front of our home was blown out. My wife narrowly missed being killed. For weeks after the bombing, my children were escorted at school. A police car was parked in front of my home for two weeks to watch for suspicious cars. Brooks and I were advised to move from our bombed homes to relocate to safer, secret addresses. Neither of us complied.

The bombing was an act of intimidation. Verbal violence followed. My opinions were threatened by anonymous phone callers. I even received the following letter from Donald Pole of the National Law Enforcement Committee:

Pardon me for pointing out that your "Left Wing" is showing. It appears from the tone of your statements that you are against any and all free thinking Americans who are thinking free. Both you and Reverend Walker seem to have shown your true colors when you spoke out against the very people whose aim it is to save America from Communist oppression.

I am not able to figure out why a man that parades in the cloak of Christianity deliberately defies all that is good and right. Have you EVER THOUGHT of the possibility that those bombs were tossed by the Zionist-Jew-Communist-Socialist forces that these free thinking Americans are seeking to expose. Perhaps this was part of a pre-determined plan to make the "Radical Right" look bad.

If you do not know now, you must surely soon become aware that the name Judaism and the name Communism are all the same 'ism. This was dramatically pointed out by Rabbi Steven Wise when he said, "Some call it Judaism, but I call it Communism." What more proof do you ask for than that. Even the Jews themselves admit it. Read the Protocols of the Learned Elders of Zion if you need more proof. Perhaps you don't need any. Perhaps you are already aware of these things. If so you are none better than they.

We of the National Law Enforcement Committee are about to expose any and all of the Communist conspirators in the church and in the Government, and I pray that we must not include you among them. God needs trusted servants, and He will smite those who parade in His name to do evil.

This letter was asking me to "repent." For what? My social ministry? My advocacy of civil rights? I love my country. **I do not love my country, right or wrong. Because I love my country, I want to right the wrongs**.

These were times when speaking for better human relations could get you charged as a Communist. McCarthyism started in the late 1940s to early 1950s. It was preceded by a congressional committee trying to burn Hollywood by accusing ten members of Communist association. The group, known as the Hollywood Ten (identified for the FBI by Ronald Reagan), was barred from work. When Joseph McCarthy entered Congress, he began lambasting everyone as a Communist. Even President Dwight Eisenhower was labeled a "dedicated Communist." Every group that wanted limelight picked up the theme.

The seeds of hate erupted. They had been sown by Fred Schwarz, the leader of the Christian anti-Communist crusade. Even Billy Graham has stopped using the term *crusade*. It means you believe or we will force you to believe—or kill you. Fred Schwarz received money from Schick Razors, Richfield Oil, and Technicolor Corporation to finance the telecast of a rally at the Hollywood Bowl in September of 1961. Schwarz was spreading the word at rallies like these all over the country.

The rally was an abomination to our right to free speech, encouraging trampling on citizen's rights. Actors were forced to admit Communist ties, and then repent, in order to be allowed to work, a modern-day Salem. Other industries followed suit. There was nothing Christian about this crusade. There was nothing constitutional about it either.

McCarthyism was a witch hunt. Constitutionality was the campaign of those who sought to defend the basic human rights of Communists, both actual and accused. Soon those defending the victims would become victims. Actress Marsha Hunt who was accused of supporting Communism by the House Un-American Committee recalls the time: "Fifty years ago I was a busy actress when suddenly I was blacklisted. No, I'd never been a Communist. Communism didn't even interest me, but I was blacklisted all the same, just for speaking out against blacklisting." She had been part of a group called the Committee for the First Amendment.

My activities at this time included being chairman of the Emergency Committee to Aid Farm Workers and active membership in the Urban League, the American Civil Liberties Union, and the National Association for the Advancement of Colored People. I served as president of the San Fernando Valley chapter of the American Association of the United Nations (AAUN) from 1959 to 1961 before Marsha Hunt took over the role. She remembers the 1950s and 1960s as "the days when it took some conviction and courage to speak in praise of the United Nations."

Communism offered to rescue mankind from acute poverty, chronic starvation, constant plague, and bewildering ignorance. The Communist theology was a political religion with a key dogma—the infallibility of the leader and the party. It believed in the wrong root of evil and the cult of the masses. The Communist theology, however, offered integration of life instead of confusion, direction instead of aimlessness, singleness of purpose instead of individualism. With the neglect of political, economic, and moral policies, which strengthen the unity and health of a non-Communist world, we were not giving it much real competition.

Communism didn't fit with my idea of Jesus, but seeking civil rights for all did. The two became synonymous, and I was accused of Communist ties by a man I'd never met. I was attacked by a campaign to get the "Communists out of the clergy."

In February of 1961, a friend and colleague, the Reverend Philip Engdahl, attended a monthly meeting of the Sun Valley Coordinating Council. The meeting was scheduled to end with a film introduced by Albert E. Saunders, then commander of the Van Nuys American Legion Post and chairman of the Counter Subversive Activities Committee of his district of the American Legion. In a letter on my behalf, Reverend Engdahl wrote,

> In his remarks [Albert Saunders] talked about the dangers of Communism and the alleged infiltration of Communism into the Churches. He stated that there are Communists in the Methodist, Presbyterian, and Lutheran Churches. There are two Lutheran ministers in the San Fernando Valley who are Communist sympathizers. One is the Pastor of Saint Matthew's Lutheran Church and founder of Pacoima Memorial Lutheran Hospital, the Rev. John Simmons.

I would not be intimidated. If we do not protect the opinions we abhor, we cannot enjoy the opinions we embrace. I demanded and received an apology for the remarks made about me without, until now, going public with his name. Meanwhile, I received anonymous threatening phone calls to my home, further accusations of Communist ties due to my involvement with the ACLU and Amnesty International.

I was no stranger to violence and threats of violence. During my campaign for mayor of Minneapolis in 1949, I was shot at two times. I was also driven off the road by someone who was after me. An insurance company executive purchased a $100,000 life insurance policy on me for my wife. It wasn't worth it!

The answer to the violence of the bombing (mine, any other, police, gangs, etc.) is going to require that people realize you CAN'T solve a problem using violence. You also can't solve problems simply by passing laws. Democracy is not a spectator sport. Men who exemplified the need for Democratic action—Martin Luther King Jr., Gandhi, Chavez—were finally destroyed in the very act of trying to be nonviolent. How, then, do we use words and acts of love in a society that just won't allow us? How do you solve the problem?

My response to the bombing of my home was three simple thoughts of William Lloyd Garrison, a witness against slavery and for freedom for all men. "I am in earnest." Not dead in earnest. Alive in earnest. My convictions are part and parcel of my integrity. They were not planted in shallow soil. Nor in rocky soil. Nor among thorns. But in good soil.

2 "I will not equivocate." That means I will not use double-talk. I will not use ambiguous language to deceive myself or anyone else concerning what I believe about in any issue of life. I have always been a controversial person. I have always been in hot water, but I know no other way to keep clean.

3 "I will be heard." I love life. My family loves life. But we will not be terrorized into silence. We will not be intimidated by violence into silence.

My good friend Hubert Humphrey sent a telegram after the bombing, saying, "I know this will not deter you in your articulate opposition to those who would destroy our democracy." Your life is determined by events, expectations, and experiences. Events happen. Your expectations of what you want to get out of each event leads to your experiences. Expectations need to be positive. I could have accepted that I was free to believe what I wanted so long as I kept to myself, that these problems of other people were for other people to solve. Instead I expected not to give into the fear that was threatening freedom.

At midnight, the night of the bombing, a number of those who witnessed the speeches, including Haskell Lazere, met at Temple Sinai. They agreed to send the following message to state, local, and national authorities: "We regard these bombings as an attempt to intimidate Americans from exercising their Constitutional guarantees of freedom of assembly and freedom of speech. We urge you to take immediate appropriate action and to issue a public statement about these acts of anarchy." Among the recipients of the telegram were President Kennedy, Attorney General Robert Kennedy, and Los Angeles mayor Samuel Yorty.

Mayor Yorty contacted me to ask what he could do. I told him to take back the statement he made approving Dr. Fred Schwarz's Christian anti-Communist crusade. Yorty then requested my presence at a press conference the morning after the bombing. I refused. I was busy. I had a frightened family and a damaged home to tend to. Yorty's people persisted, and a car was sent for me. I was upset to find the press conference already complete when I arrived. Yorty then began to lecture myself and the other "guests," telling us we were wrong. I stood up and said, "Mayor Yorty, I resent that I was called down here only to find that the press conference was over. You used me as a tool."

Drew Pearson, writer for the *Washington Post*, came out the night after the press conference to write an article that would take on national significance and grab the attention of Mayor Yorty. Shortly after the article was printed, Pearson informed me that he and I were being sued over a statement I made that Pearson included in the article. Yorty made himself out to be a liberal. My comments (or, perhaps, Yorty's unwillingness to respond to my comment at the press conference) exposed his right-wing side.

Sam Yorty claimed I'd accused him of being an accessory to the Fred Schwarz rally. The lawsuit never even hit local papers and was only published in San Bernardino. Sam Yorty was trying to burn me without the local public finding out by suing me through a reporter in Washington! The actual printed statement was the same response given directly to Yorty at his press conference. I had said, "You can take back that statement you made approving Dr. Fred Schwarz and his Christian anti-Communist crusade." The case was ridiculous, like a child getting back at another child. Pearson offered to handle the whole thing, but the case was dropped. Meanwhile, Mayor Yorty never accepted my many offers to an open, public debate.

Drew Pearson wasn't my only support. During a meeting of the Senate just days after the bombing, Senator Thomas Kuchel (Republican, California) turned the floor over to my friend (and then, acting majority leader) Hubert Humphrey. I was able to obtain a copy of the congressional record including Humphrey's statements, calling attention to the danger of that time: "I think it is the duty of Congress and of other public officials who have taken an oath to uphold the Constitution to call the attention of the American public to the danger to our democratic and republican institutions that exists in this kind of extremism and this kind of violence.

"[T]his extreme radical right wing, by its self-appointed, super-duper patriotism, by its constantly reiterated antagonism to Communism, has a tendency to attract followers, without the people knowing they are being caught up in the web of a Fascist movement which does nothing but aid and abet the cause of destruction, disorder, and totalitarianism."

The record continues with other senators concurring with Humphrey's statements. The incident needed attention, mainly to educate. Ignorance is easy. It is easy to get caught up in the support of a movement with so much propaganda. People needed exposure to other viewpoints.

Hate incited the bombing, but love and hope came out of it. There was a strengthening of the relationships of family, friends, citizens, political leaders, colleagues, and members of the church. Out of the bombings surfaced many more people who agreed the fear had to stop. There was a need for a nonpartisan event. We got busy planning a rally against the bombings with a sponsoring committee consisting of college presidents, civic officials, businessmen, Hollywood stars, and leading clergymen from most of the major religious groups. The public was well represented. We also secured

Senate speakers representing both major parties—Clifford Case (R, New Jersey) and Eugene McCarthy (D, Minnesota).

We chose the date of April 12, the anniversary of the death of Franklin D. Roosevelt. "The only thing we have to fear is fear itself." He spoke these words in the midst of the greatest economic crisis we have ever experienced. Regardless of party affiliation, these words gave to all Americans, and the world of freemen, courage in that hour.

An estimated five thousand people attended our town hall meeting for democracy at the Shrine Auditorium. The response of the people was to educate and support the United Nations and the American Civil Liberties Union. Those in public office agreed to the strengthening of laws and public policies that affirm our freedoms. An editorial in the *Christian Century* called the event "liberating," citing that it was "both representative and reasonable in the highest democratic tradition."

Excerpt from the INSTALLATION ADDRESS OF REV. JOHN G.
SIMMONS as Pacoima Memorial Lutheran Hospital administrator
at Valley Lutheran Church
February 18, 1962

Seriously, I, too, was taken aback when asked to make an address of substance
at my own installation. Upon more sober reflection, I decided it would give
me an opportunity to organize and give voice to ideas and commitments
that are mine as I accept this new ministry of administration.

Time since the night of February 1 has been at a premium. I have been
preoccupied in dealing with my thoughts and emotions and those of my
family. In the larger context of the community and in the narrower context
of the hospital community, the terror bombing of our home has absorbed
my time in meeting a multitude of problems. Therefore this address will
not be my very best. I am sure you will understand.

The decision which I made to leave my parish ministry of pulpit and altar
was an agonizing experience. I dearly love the members of the fellowship of
St. Matthew's. I served with them for over ten years in an exciting ministry
of social concern in the ministry.

Religion and health and healing have historically been interrelated and
integrated. Religion and the uniting of men together in the bundle of life
with the Lord God is one of the biblical expressions of health and salvation.
From the dawn of history, the holy man was a medicine man, the healer,
the one to whom the sick and diseased person looked for help.

The temple and the church were both places of healing. The Christian
Church inherited the healing tradition from Judaism. When a Jew was ill, it
was the rabbi to whom he went rather than the doctor. The rabbi anointed
him with oil and prayed over him. The sick went to the holy man. It is still
so among primitive people.

Religion was the way of life. It included the foods to be eaten and the
foods to be avoided. This was the way the person honored his Creator with
his body. Likewise the food of his mind was carefully prescribed as part of
his whole response to God.

There developed in the Roman and Greek civilization as religious-
centered and motivated medical practice. You have seen on medical buildings
a strange-looking symbol. The serpent is the symbol of the Greek and Roman
god of healing. Temples to Aesculapius, were built. He was called "savior of
the world", "the lord healer." According to the record, Aesculapius tamed
serpents who were supposed to be the incarnation of the gods. The sick

people would sleep at night in the temples of Aesculapius, and if one of the tame serpents glided over them, they would be healed.

Every doctor takes an oath, known as the Hippocratic oath. Hippocrates was so respected that his words were used by the Church historian Eusebius and applied to Jesus:

> Like some excellent physician in order to cure the sick, He examines what is repulsive, handles sores, and reaps pain himself from the sufferings of others.

There came a tragic split in the early centuries between religion and medicine that has not, to this day, been completely healed. Both religion and medicine were responsible. As late as the nineteenth century, Sir James Simpson, a devout Christian, had to fight against certain sections of the church when he proposed to use chloroform to ease the pain of childbirth.

I am excited at the role of the hospital in the healing and health of the community in all its social relationships; the social sickness, illness, and disease are the major health problems of our generation. These diseased social relationships often produce body, mind, and spirit disease, illness, and sickness. Social wounds do not always bleed before our eyes. They are often internal injuries of spirit and of mind. But they will out! The prejudice, hostility, hate, envy, and fear we have for our fellow men who differ in any way from us is a cancer. It does produce sickness, disease, illness. This is a frontier that I want to explore with you during the years ahead.

The healing community of the hospital must move toward the healing of the social sicknesses and diseases in the community with commitment to seek to prevent social sickness and not merely to cure or to be content with curing superficially. The whole man—body, mind, and spirit—must be made whole again; if not, we shall be torn apart, man set against his fellow man. The creating and sharing of a common unity of purpose.

CHAPTER FIVE

Pacifist, Not Passive

In 1950, I had given a keynote address at the South Dakota Democratic Convention, just a few years after the successful merger of the Democratic and Farmer Labor parties in Minnesota. My main point was to educate both the farmer and wage earner on the proposition that they belong together politically just as they are interdependent and interrelated economically. There had been a determined attempt to create misunderstanding between the farmer and wage earner. When strikes occurred, big business played the farmer against the wage earner to the hurt of both.

Problems were similar when I moved to California. The Mexican bracero system was implemented by Public Law 78 and was a foreign contract labor system thrusting into the economy and the American community a massive pliant, readily exploitable, foreign-captive labor force. The bracero system was not a system of freemen. It rested upon desperate hunger in the rural area of Mexico. As an alternative to starvation, it offered men servitude.

I appreciate Cesar Chavez for his commitment to nonviolently organizing the poor, for his love of life shaped by sacrifice, and for his love of the God who daily strengthened him for the struggle. Cesar Chavez was born March 31, 1927. He attended sixty-five schools, but never graduated from high school. He died struggling for what his mother and father had lost—Bruce Church Inc. owned the land that once was Chavez Family farmland, land that Cesar believed had been unjustly taken from them.

Chavez was anti-bracero. He once told the very sad story of Don Pedro. He was too old to work in the fields as he had for over twenty-five years. He worked for contractors in Arizona and in the Central Valley. Don Pedro said, "Last week I went to the social security office, and they told me I have no benefits, but I know the *contratistas* (contractors) always took money out of my check for social security. These filthy contractors stole my money. I have nothing now, nothing to live with." In early 1993, *60 Minutes* told the story of contractors in Florida. "Workers were paid with company 'dollars' that could only be spent at the contractor's concession stands. They were charged exorbitant prices—up to $2.00 for a can of soda. And worse, these men were literally imprisoned by the contractor, their green-cards taken away so they couldn't leave until the harvest was over."

Cesar Chavez fought for the likes of Ruffino Contreras, who was killed in a legitimate strike. There were strikebreakers present. The judge William Lehnhardt (whose wife and son were among the strikebreakers!) decided that the UFW of America must pay $2.5 million to the powerful growers. Lehnhardt ruled that Ruffino's killers should not be prosecuted and that the $2.5 million be paid before the UFW could appeal the decision. This is not justice!

Justice is a higher value than *empowerment* and *representation*. Cesar Chavez lived simply and made us uneasy in our lifestyles. He lived with integrity. Chavez embodied moral leadership for minorities and the poor farmworkers. He was self-educated in public libraries through the writings of Gandhi and John Steinbeck. He organized workers. He registered Mexican American voters. Cesar was more, much more, than an image on a stamp or a paid holiday. He had the courage to live his faith, his active life for the poor, and to speak truth to the oppressors in the war against the workers and their children. They were more than braceros—they were his friends.

The rights of the braceros were violated. We took advantage of their misfortune. Caesar Chavez was trying to get organized with no support from the Catholic Church. Mexicans worked farms in Ventura County, but all the signs posted were in English. That is an injustice! I worked for and became chairman of the Emergency Committee to Aid Farm Workers in 1960.

While I was chairman of the Emergency Committee to Aid Farm Workers, I gave speeches. After one such speech, a woman named Elizabeth Longbottom came to me as a committee representative. She told us she was the keeper of the books of the braceros. She admitted she got paid by the growers for falsifying the records. We immediately filed an action, and though we got denials, we eventually took them (the growers) to federal court. We told our story before the House Committee with Elizabeth Longbottom's testimony. The growers were fined. I don't know if they were ever actually made to pay.

Another problem was the inability of braceros to defend themselves through the formation of a union. The National Labor Board would offer the workers an opportunity to vote on the formation of a union and would set the date a month or so later where the men were working in the San Joaquin Valley. When it was time to vote, the workers had been moved to the Imperial Valley and did not have the transportation to get back and vote. We obtained an OEO grant and used the funds to bus the workers back to the San Joaquin Valley the day of the vote, strangely a Sunday.

In 1963, we sought to phase out Public Law 78. There were other consequences of the bracero system. It made the braceros victims, forced small farmers out of business, and depressed the living standards of all American farmworkers. The average hourly farm wage rate in California in 1961 was $1.25 per hour. This rate did not truly reflect the wages of general field workers as the average included foremen and skilled equipment operators. *Economic violence is not paying a living wage.*

Additionally, small farms began to disappear, putting many family businesses out of business. Larger land holdings were falling into the hands of fewer owners. The bracero system allowed for the monopolization of farms, making the owners more like large corporations than the small farms we think of. Finally, when braceros retired, they wanted homes for themselves. When they retired, however, we began to treat them as illegal immigrants. The Rural Development got all unions to participate and built affordable housing for retired braceros.

Certainly it was not the braceros' intentions to be used as an instrument to displace U.S. workers. Yet our system treated them with shame. I was chairman of the Emergency Committee to Aid Farm Workers for ten years. I've tried to figure out how I could be most effective when I could personally do something about it. That's why I've been involved in civil rights and liberties addressed to a specific situation.

"The truest act of courage, the strongest act of manliness is to sacrifice ourselves for others in a totally non-violent struggle for justice. To be a man is to suffer for others. God help us to be men." This quote by Caesar Chavez speaks to man's need to be a part of a community and how communities need to support one another.

As administrator of Pacoima Memorial Lutheran Hospital, I found the hospital had limited resources, human and financial. It was limited because of the geographical cul-de-sac in which it was located. It was limited because the community had a high percentage of educationally, economically, and racially disadvantaged persons. Limited financial resources also limited the human resources of personnel with the credentials to do the jobs.

Public education is essential to a viable and continuing democratic society. Public education has enabled people to break out of a feudal rigid caste or guild system by enabling them to qualify themselves for different positions outside the family caste in which they were born. Public education is the primary force making equality of opportunity a reality because it qualifies people to work according to their interest and ability.

Pacoima Memorial Lutheran Hospital lacked qualified people willing to work in the hospital. And unemployment levels in Pacoima were among the highest in all of Los Angeles county. You have to be involved with the community if you're going to be a community hospital. The health of the community includes more than the physical health of its people. It includes the political, economic, educational, mental, social, and religious health. I had to come up with a solution. That solution was Casa Loma College.

Casa Loma College opened in 1966. At the time, such a nontraditional school was something many snickered at. The idea was to provide opportunities for even high school dropouts, so a diploma was not required for enrollment. You could earn your diploma while training in the medical field. And since knowledge is more than you can acquire from reading and lectures, our students were given practical experiences on the hospital floor. Sixty percent of the ten-month training is in the hospital. The very first day that a person has to carry a bedpan they know if they really want to become a vocational nurse!

The struggles of the braceros and the beginning of Casa Loma College have much in common. We live in a time of violence—bombings, kidnappings, murders. There is, however, another kind of violence affecting far more people. It is the violence of unemployment that destroys the hope of the unemployed and his family. It is the violence of chronic insecurity as occurs in poor communities, which destroys persons. It is the violence of unequal laws and injustice that makes people unemployable.

An initiative in education was passed in 2001 called the *No Child Left Behind Act.* Despite its good intentions, this act excludes a major chunk of the population. It is designed to improve the future for many children, but what about everybody else? What about adults, the elderly, the mentally ill? Health is complete physical, mental, spiritual, and social well-being. The lack of employment, inadequate housing, inadequate diet, as well as loneliness and frustration, all result in disease and injury to persons.

What's it all about, John? I propose a new act, the No PERSON Left Behind Act. People fail to see the immorality of war, of poverty. People are more willing to practice charity (feeding the hungry, for example) than to engage in the practice of ensuring *just treatment* of all. Every person—man, woman, and child—should be entitled to have an education, train for a job, have a job at a living (not a minimum) wage, and own a home (not given to them). They also deserve the right to voice their opinions and vote for candidates that will make this happen.

We believe poor people are dumb and/or lazy, but most simply lack skills and resources. Society is controlled by corporations who buy politicians through generous campaign contributions. Members of Congress are busier returning favors when they should be concerned with the state of our country's people. It is immoral.

I remember one encounter with someone of the born again theology in Chicago. As I got off the L train, I was met by a stranger. He looked me in the eye and asked, "Have you found the Lord?" I answered, sinfully annoyed, "I didn't know He was lost." Both of us went our separate ways. I wish that I understood then that we were both wrong!

I was encouraged to examine the crusades historically. They began after Constantine made Christianity the only religion of the Roman Empire. It changed from a servant church to a male domination control corporation with a hierarchy of popes and cardinals. Creeds and confessions were to be obeyed. Failure to comply resulted in excommunication, heresy trials, and in many cases, killing of the heretic.

The emphasis on evangelism should not be salvation by formula. When Constantine made Christianity the religion of the empire, he decided on a form of domination by the popes, men only, which the state would enforce—the church became an arm of the state. Men made all the rules, and the state enforced them. The hierarchy decided on creeds and beliefs. The Apostles' Creed did not emerge at the crucifixion of Jesus. It was not put into the official doctrine until the end of the third century.

Women were victims of the system. They were demeaned and controlled by men. They were men's property. Men controlled their property, their bodies. A woman could not even ask for a divorce. Only men could divorce their wives. Men were not punished, responsible, or accountable.

Three of my most important influences were women. They made me what I am because they were supportive, good critics from different vantage points. I only had one sister growing up, Jeannette. At a young age, Jeannette did things with me to help Dad, like taking shorthand and typing. She was a Harvard graduate, very intelligent. She never married. She worked for the World Health Organization and went to Indonesia. She was a professor at Harvard at one time and president of the Society of Public Health Educators. She was a good help and an advisor to me in my various projects, changing jobs or taking time off to be close to me. Jeannette helped with my campaign for mayor. She was very helpful while working for the Tennessee Valley Authority. She was like a second mother to my children and retired to Northern California to be near them. Now that she is in assisted living with a memory disorder, my kids still take her to dinner.

My wife Mary Jane and I never had a fight. She did decide our life was too much for her, and we separated. We shared an attorney through all aspects of the divorce until we appeared in front of the judge (at which point we just got another friend to represent her!). I was supportive financially, and she always supported me! We remained friends. We kept in close contact until she died of cancer.

My wife Bethene and I are married now thirty-six years. She was director of nursing at Pacoima Memorial Lutheran Hospital. She had been divorced for fifteen years and had five children (eight kids between us!) with whom I have always had a good relationship.

My wife Bethene and I

She took responsibility for me and worked in the community in Southern California where we lived (and still live). She quit the hospital so no one could be critical of decisions either of us made (I was administrator). She was always good counsel and brought good experience in dealing with people. She was also a stabilizing influence.

With Constantine came the theme of control and domination by the ecclesiasts. During this time, only men were ordained. Only men filled the roles of pope, bishop, and layperson. The only role for women was that of a nun. It left women answering to males in a subservient role. Lutherans have only practiced ordaining women for close to forty years. Presbyterians are still trying. Catholics are nowhere close.

When the Depression came, women were not employed. In the beginning, my father was part of a group that marched on Washington. His group insisted upon having opportunities for women to work, as more and more men went off to war. There was resistance.

My generation was applauded for what I consider minimal advancement by the way of equality for women. Women still have limited opportunity. Their social security is about two-thirds the amounts of men like I. They are still paid less for doing equal work. Education, a field dominated by women, is still one of the lowest paid professions. Poverty has become feminized; two out of three adults living in poverty are women. Society pushes women into a clinging vine role while autonomy and independence are given to men.

The most common crime in human relations is not against white, black, brown, or gay and lesbian. It is domestic violence. It is men against their wives and children. Male dominance is still a fact. Over 50 percent of fathers fail to obey court orders to pay child and spousal support. The laws that have been enacted to reduce male dominance and give hope to spouses cannot be implemented.

Individual women may get a fair share, but the truth is many women are still challenging their gender roles in the home. A marriage should be a partnership, a true partnership. Each person is valued for their own position. Each person has equal say. Only in partnership is there power.

The terms *domination* and *partnership*, as I have come to use them, come from the work of social scientist Riane Eisler. Two of her most significant works are *The Chalice and the Blade* and *The Power of Partnership*. Eisler uses the terms *domination* and *partnership* to refer to systems of living. Her work started a whole movement called the Center of Partnership Studies. She has received a variety of awards for peace and now teaches at the California Institute of Integral Studies.

Domination extends to all life. Riane Eisler discusses the ranking of human beings—men over women, clergy over laity, white people over colored people, rich over poor, etc., as the essential and most fundamental characteristic of what she calls the "dominator system." The dominator theory, according to Eisler, is man-made and man-controlled. Domination and control—that is what the Christian Church became under Constantine. We now rank just about everything and everybody. This system of domination then determines how we think by creating stereotypes. The ranking teaches us what is desired and what is not.

The domination system plays an inhibiting role. Those in power stay in power because the rest of us are kept distracted, arguing over whose God is the true God, or if there is a God at all. No policy that is based upon control of others can possibly be a God-ordained way. Our arrogance is needed to support the machinery of the church. Political and personal relationships based on domination result in misery and violence. Positive community change is hindered.

The problem is that we are too individualistic. It is not what you can get out of it—it's what the community needs. What *I want* out of this life is not the way. The system where every man for himself is really a put-down to everyone who doesn't adopt that philosophy is a system that locks oppressed people against each other.

GREED

T.S. Farisani

If there will be a third world war,
A war that will be won by losers
Losers winning everything but their life, it's
Life of greed.
If East and West shall never agree,
And negotiations drag on and on
While wars drain their coffers, it's
Life of greed.
If the North shall grow richer and richer,
And the South poorer and poorer, it's
Life of greed.
If millionaires conceive billionaires,
And beggars crowd the earth with paupers,
it's
Life of greed.
If Christians build cathedrals for pianos huge
and large,
And fellow believers can't buy a Bible, it's
Life of greed.
If two people occupy a six room house,
While four spend a winter night in the street
below,
Christ must surely die again!
To enliven consciences buried in greed.

Greed has infected millions. It has infected every segment of our lives. Fairness is obsolete. We live in a society in which "me-ism" rules. We have covetousness and greed taught and practiced at every level. Do whatever you can to acquire whatever you can for yourself, your family, your group. If the pursuit of happiness means that I have more than you, it's a sin. My happiness stops at the end of my nose. It is spiritual crisis—affluence, not influence; control, not sharing.

Greed and covetousness are sins. Greed is manipulative. Greed undermines all virtues. It is destructive of love. It destroys communities. Look at our country. The ratio of pay to executives versus their staff has been as high as 271 dollars to 1! Salaries, stock options, and golden parachutes as compensation to executives even as companies have begun to go out of existence. Sports figures, lobbyists, and politicians are all involved. And charity is not a substitute. Getting a tax break for a charitable donation is not unselfish love.

Our government and our Congress have the responsibility to confront the greedy in business. The church has the responsibility to speak openly, to point the finger at the greedy in business, including itself. The church is a corporation run from the top by men. I have been criticized by both the religious establishment and by political leaders and groups because of my insistence that they need to be challenged. It is all people's right to take part in causes related to justice and peace.

The key word in the Christian faith, in any faith, should be *community*. Jesus was a heretic when he proclaimed that we must live in love, forgiveness, and joy. He preached a Gospel of community. He rejected hierarchy. He rejected the idea that popes, priests, and nobles were favorites of God. Jesus did not mean for us to be divided.

Excerpt from "ANONYMOUS DISCIPLES"
Reverend John G. Simmons
First Lutheran Church
Los Angeles, California
April 29, 1979
Luke 24

> "The Disciples from Emmaus were telling
> the Eleven about their experience."

Obviously with Judas having hanged himself, there were eleven disciples left. But it says, "As the two Disciples from Emmaus were telling their Story to the Eleven." Obviously we don't know their names. About four or five weeks ago when I was preparing the Easter season sermons, this verse jumped out at me. Obviously, these two were anonymous disciples. I began to think of the number of people to whom all of us are indebted, who do the kind things anonymously. Most of the nations of the world have a "tomb of the unknown soldier, known only to God." Look at the Bible or the hymnbook, and you'll discover many, many anonymous disciples. This is God's story, and the persons are not the center of the story—God is. He knows our names, and that is important.

We want our names to be known, and we do everything to make that happen. It is part of our continuing struggle against our anxieties concerning our death. The hymn "Adeste Fidelis" or "Come Thy Almighty King" or "O Holy God, Thy Name We Praise," "The Strife Is O'er, the Victory Is Won"—their authors are unknown. And I thought to myself, that's who we are—"*anonymous disciples.*"

The Old Testament is filled with all kinds of illustrations of unknown disciples of God. The story of Elijah who was told by God to go into Kerith and there he would find a home where a widow lived with her son. And sure enough, Elijah found the home with the widow and her son. In the midst of this experience, he gets the widow to take what little she has (because of the drought) to make him something to eat. We don't know her name—known only by God. What an amazing story. We don't know the names of many people in the Bible who helped Jesus. "There is a lad here with bread and fish"—no name, but then the miracle of feeding five thousand people. Or the experience of Jesus saying to His disciples, "Go into the city and there you'll find a man [another anonymous disciple] who has a donkey and tell him to borrow it for the Peace Parade." We don't know the person who furnished the Upper Room where Jesus went for Passover and instituted the Lord's Supper. It was probably that same Upper Room where the disciples met that first Easter evening, frightened and afraid of being caught and put to death. It was that same Upper Room, eight days later, that Thomas came and met "his Lord and his God."

I think it may be helpful for us to take a look at ourselves. We are among the anonymous disciples in our time. We have a responsibility to do what we can in witness to Jesus Christ. Paul says that he was indebted to a great host of people. The book of Hebrews in the twelfth chapter says, "Therefore, seeing that we are surrounded by a great crowd of witnesses, let us run with patience the race set for us, looking for Jesus, the Author and Finisher of our faith." The whole focus of God's story in the Bible from beginning to end is not all of us individually named—the focus is on God. It's God's story of His struggle with His people, seeking to make them disciples.

I had an interesting experience after World War II on a number of occasions with Bishop Hans Lilje. He resisted Hitler in World War II and spent his time in a concentration camp, in prison, or under house arrest. I remember his telling of a prison experience. He thought the next day was the day he would be put to death. There was an air alarm, and the prison, of course, was put in complete darkness. The guards had gone clattering down the staircase, and he heard them talking as they approached the air-raid shelter. He said, "I thought that everything was going to be all over if they bombed. It was as quiet as death." He said, "Suddenly and silently, both bolts on my cell door were pushed back, and a man entered and signaled me to silence—one of those responsible for watching me." He said quietly to the bishop, "Don't you think we too understand Gethsemane and the Cross better than ever before." That's "anonymous discipleship."

Oscar Wilde, in a book of more modern time called *De Profundis*, tells of his experience of being led handcuffed between two policemen from prison into the court. A friend of his came to watch, and as he passed by him, his friend just tipped his hat. Oscar Wilde said the memory of that little lovely silent act of love has unsealed for me all the wells of pity.

God is looking for anonymous disciples. It's amazing what happens in the world of our relationships when people don't care who gets credit for it. We need the spontaneous response, not the calculated or seeking credit response, in our lives.

There's a second thought I want to suggest. Namely, that the world is made livable by anonymous disciples—the anonymous disciples of peace and love. This means all of us. The world is made livable by anonymous disciples—not those thirsty for power who misuse it and abuse it, but those who respond because the love of Christ compels them. Too many look at the future believing they can do nothing. We dare not resign ourselves to accepting the fatalistic philosophy of "there is nothing we can do"—that what we do won't make any difference. You see, that's not the question. The question is what are you doing with the stubborn ounces of your weight to tip the scale for a way of love and peace and understanding, acceptance and concern for other people besides yourself without caring about getting credit for it in klieg lights or in church bulletins!

CHAPTER SIX

The Cult of Reagan

Now, I need to backpedal just a little. I'll be discussing a man whose name still makes my heart rate go up, even at the age of ninety-two, even long after he has passed. His name comes to mind when I think of poor, underfunded education systems and deficiencies in hospital care.

I met Ronald Reagan in Des Moines, Iowa, in 1934. I caddied at the Des Moines Golf and Country Club. My sister worked in the clubhouse. She saw Reagan. She remembers he was busy looking at the women rather than anything else. He often visited on ladies' day. Reagan was a sportscaster. He made up baseball stories, dramatizing games over the wire service for the entertainment of Chicago Cubs fans in Des Moines and beyond. He was good at it.

Ronald Reagan told people his goal was to be an actor. It's fair to say Reagan always wanted to be in a power position. It wasn't how good an actor you were. Power was being in the Screen Actors Guild. He sought the nonpaying job to head the Screen Actors Guild. In order to do this, he had to get rid of some people. Over seventy people were obstacles to his career. Scott Herald, son of Robert Herald, owner of the San Jose Mercury News, used the Freedom of Information Act to expose that from 1942, Reagan had been a confidential informant for the Federal Bureau of Investigation. Using the code name T-Ten, he informed on all his opponents in the Screen Actors Guild. Reagan labeled them Communists to have them blacklisted.

Reagan had power by virtue of his position—power to make and unmake other actors. Those he informed on lost their careers, including my close friend Marsha Hunt and her husband, Robert Presnell. Additionally, prosecutor Ed Meese tried to have Scott Herald fired over the article exposing Reagan, but information released a few years later by a confidential informant for the FBI confirmed that Reagan had informed against the Hollywood Ten, most of whom were members of the Screen Actors Guild.

Reagan married Jane Wyman, an actress, after realizing it might be good for his career. They had two children, neither of whom liked him because he never spent any time with them. He made a couple of B movies. In a biography of James Garner, by Raymond Strait, Garner is quoted as saying, "Oh, Ronnie, Ronnie, isn't he wonderful? Listen, I was vice president of the Screen Actors Guild when he was its president, and we used to tell him what to say. He can talk around a subject better than anyone in the world. He never had an original thought that I know of, and we go back a lot of years. You realize I could have been your president?" I guess Hollywood wasn't the place for a puppet.

Reagan and Wyman divorced. Then Reagan met and married Nancy Davis. Her father was a very conservative doctor, and was conservative politically. Reagan gave up his "liberal" views—he had been a Democrat for a while though he was to the right of Attila the Hun! He made speeches for the American Medical Association for which he was paid handsomely. He read their scripts. In the 1960s, he spoke about how if the legislation establishing Medicare was passed, we'd all be telling our children and grandchildren decades hence what freedom used to be like. Reagan was also the spokesman for General Electric. He received hundreds of thousands of dollars to share GE's views, such as no tax for the rich.

Ronald Reagan focused on image over facts. (He was quoted saying, "Facts are stupid." He once said trees cause pollution). Reagan wanted to be photographed on his front step in full uniform kissing his wife good-bye—excellent acting. Reagan told Itsaf Shamir that he was in uniform for four years and told Simon Wiesenthal that he had been involved in liberating the Jewish victims of the Holocaust. He was never even in the service! It was a lie, a wrong thing to do. Reagan instead gave us jelly beans. He carried them around in his pocket.

The immoral acts of Reagan are lost behind his larger-than-life Hollywood persona. The cult around Reagan was successful because he was pictured favorably. Everybody saw this good-looking guy and excellent speaker. Reagan never understood the legislative process. Reagan's policies transformed our country into a moral jungle. Public and private deceit, graft, and corruption existed both in the White House and on Wall Street. Greed was cast as free enterprise.

Ronald Reagan had always been opposed to civil rights. He never wanted the 1964 Civil Rights Act to be implemented. He never agreed to the Martin Luther King Jr. holiday in California. He only had use for women who could advance him and attacked the feminist movement by being against the Equal Rights Amendment. He called welfare people "bums who need to get back to work" and created the image of "welfare queens" as women who picked up their checks in Cadillacs. He never mentioned AIDS, speaking like it was a sort of measles that would go away. He quieted the attorney general from any public commentary of the AIDS epidemic. Reagan's appointments of Supreme Court Justices were appalling. William Rehnquist had a record of discrimination, and Anthony Kennedy was a member of a club that explicitly excluded minorities and women.

Those were moral decisions. Ronald Reagan had NO ethics as related to the way he treated people. What constitutes an ethical position on these matters? It is not how the law is or is not written, it is how you treat the subject and the people. Ronald Reagan attended Eureka College, a Disciple of Christ school that trained people for ministry. (I attended Drake University, another Disciple of Christ school. We were fraternity brothers as members of Tau Kappa Epsilon.) He was not active at any church and never got around to dealing with any of that. Reagan was always in support of the domination system believing that the people in power make decisions about religious life.

Reagan was elected governor when there was a fight at the University of California at Berkeley. He ran against Pat Brown and promised to "clean up the mess at Berkeley." He claimed that the faculty at the university was too permissive and supportive of students protesting against the invasion of Cambodia. Ed Meese was told to "get those guys." Reagan made blistering speeches about the chancellor of UC Berkeley, Clark Kerr, charging him as a leftist and accusing him of having people who were really Communists. He got the National Guard out to quiet the protestors and had Clark Kerr fired.

Additionally, Reagan's campaign against those on welfare helped him win the 1966 election. He was governor of California from 1967 until 1975. I was opening a new type of college (Casa Loma), a new opportunity for those in need. The people of Pacoima, many of whom were on Reagan's so-called lazy list, needed access to opportunity. Reagan was making access to education a difficulty unless you had money. I was making access to education a possibility even without a high school diploma.

Reagan smuggled the Vietnam experience into our accepted American wars!

Then, for eight years, he was the president of our country. Reagan was the epitome of the public relations industry in control of the corporate elites. The use of polling was not to understand public opinion but rather to sell its policies in spite of public opinion. What's wrong? That turns the governing process into a sales campaign and makes a mockery of democracy.

People were sold on Contra Aid. Reagan knew of the Iran-Contra scandal operation. The Sandinista government, compared with our allies in Central America, did not slaughter its population. That's a fact. Nicaragua is the only country that tried to direct resources to the poor and that tried for social justice. Guatemala and El Salvador were war-slaughter terrorist states. In the 1980s, they slaughtered 150,000 of their own citizens with U.S. support and enthusiasm. Honduras' government was rich and robbed the poor.

After 241 marines died in Lebanon on October 23, 1983, Reagan ordered U.S. forces to invade Grenada in order to protect 800 students in a medical college. We lost 18 Americans, 45 Grenadans, and 24 Cubans in that invasion. There was nothing really wrong, no threat to the United States. It was a way to show we were winners, another B-rated film of Reagan's.

A firewall was built around Reagan in the Iran-Contra conspiracy and the cover-up. People seem to have forgotten the mess involving Oliver North. Reagan was involved with those indicted (and later pardoned by George Bush Sr.) in the Iran-Contra scandal—Meese, Deaver, Nosinger, Poindexter, and MacFarlane to name a few. The truth is more people were indicted (53) and convicted (43) in the Reagan administration that in any administration before, and any since. Oliver North ran the Contra Cocaine for Guns conspiracy. Anyone who would declare Olie North a hero is either crazy or has another agenda!

Reaganism empowered and enabled greed, arrogance, neglect, and hypocrisy. He was a storyteller and became known as the Teflon president because blame never stuck on him. There is so much more that is glossed over. Ronald Reagan

- opposed Martin Luther King Jr. Day, saying he might yet be proved a Communist;
- called the court ordered school district integration plan by Los Angeles judge Alfred Gitelson *ridiculous*;
- opposed affirmative action hiring policies when he was governor;

- dismissed feminism as *boredom* more than oppression;
- mocked environmentalists during the controversy over the fate of the California redwood forests with the statement, "When you've seen one tree, you've seen them all";
- was given the power to edit, reduce, or eliminate money without the substance of a bill. In 1969, when the state legislature passed a fifteen-million-dollar school lunch bill, the governor cut it 90 percent to $500,000;
- declared ketchup a vegetable to justify school lunch budget cuts;
- opposed money—$500,000,000—to close the educational opportunity gap;
- fired PATCO Air Traffic controllers en masse when they went on strike for better pay and working conditions;
- closed state mental hospitals, as governor, labeling psychiatrists "headshrinkers." Thousands lost their jobs;
- didn't pay state income taxes in 1970. He was indicted for perjury;
- closed the nine University of California campuses during protests over the invasion of Cambodia. During this time, he is quoted as saying, "If it takes a bloodbath, let's get it over with no more apprehension";
- called for more force against those he called "mad dogs" during the 1967 rebellion in the ghettos;
- believed that "homeless people are homeless by choice";
- sold arms to Khumeni and funded the contras;
- courted Saddam Hussein even after his use of chemical weapons;
- believed that nuclear war is winnable and appointed military officials who agreed;
- helped the anti-Semitic junta of Argentina;
- backed the military governments in El Salvador and Guatemala that massacred civilians;
- helped Chilean dictator Augusto Pinchet;
- told Israeli prime minister Yitzak Shamir that he had actually assisted in the liberation of the Nazi death camps;
- censored news, that is, the 1983 invasion of Grenada.

The list could go on. The media was not critical of Reagan because the people didn't want to hear it. The Iran-Contra scandal alone made Watergate "like a penny waiting for change."

The history of America is not true, but Reagan pushed that stuff—the United States' way of life is the way of life for everybody. Films of the American past made during Reagan's time (including many John Wayne titles) are nothing but propaganda. Films such as *Spirit of the American Past, Gone with the Wind, Dodge City*, and other so-called classics are an attempt to paper over a history that is not good and make America out to be something that it is not.

Nancy Reagan decided that Ronald was going to be famous—the beginning of the Cult of Reagan. Ronald Reagan is now lauded as worthy of being the fifth face on Mount Rushmore. An airport was named for him despite the PATCO incident. He already has buildings, parks, post offices, and courthouses in his name. Now his image is replacing local heroes in some areas, for example the Thomas Starr King statue. When asked about running for office, his reply was, "I don't know. I've never played a governor before." He IS a good actor. My friend and colleague, Stan Olson, had this to share just after Reagan's death:

> We knew it was coming. We just didn't know when. Alzheimer's wins every time. It's just a matter of time. Such has been the ever so slow time bomb that had its grip on the life of one of our past presidents. And then the news came: The Great Communicator had died. Ronald Reagan had been set free from the imprisoning disease that had robbed him, and us, of his presence these past ten years.

> The grand show this week has swallowed up the media and rivals anything that Hollywood could have concocted. What a production! It made me decide never again to put down liturgical wizards. Here, for the world to see, we watched the practiced perfection of countless specialists in the military. Their sole purpose has been to be trained in their specialized functions in case they were ever needed. And they performed to perfection. Not everyone in the military serves in fox holes or swabs the decks of battleships. Maybe I could use a few of them when my day arrives.

> What a funeral! The very term "high Church" faded into and amateur show compared with the military protocol wizards.

Where have they been hiding all this time waiting and yet practicing for such an occasion. It made me thankful that the military soaked up so many of them thus keeping them from overpowering religious ceremonies. They are safely kept busy where they can do little harm.

Years ago when Ronald Reagan was nothing but the governor of this state we would go on our vacation to our cabin on the banks of the Cache la Poudre River above Fort Collins, Colorado. Most vacationers on the river are from the Midwest. Mid-westerners love to escape from the hot billiard table flatness of their blazing hot summers. They often outnumbered Californians fifty to one. When these fellow vacationers would discover that we were from California a certain mystical awe would descend upon them and they would say, "What's it like having God as your governor?"

Well, they didn't exactly use those words but what they expressed was as un-mistakenly clear. When they heard [my wife] and I express doubts and even down right pessimism concerning our governor they were shocked beyond belief. He was as close to a deity they had ever seen or heard in the flesh. We were obviously not numbered among the many saved. Armageddon would be our fate.

That near divine mantle was evident this week as an adoring nation lined the walks around the capital, crowded every street where the casket would pass and stood for endless hours waiting for a chance to catch a fleeting glimpse. Critics or doubters had to keep far away from the adoring mobs if they valued their lives. Unbelievers were anathema.

I began wondering if the procession needed to be stopped and the casket opened to see if a body was still inhabiting it. Had he already been assumed to heaven? In the Book of Revelation there is the scene of the 144,000 who will be saved. Does anyone doubt for a minute that our former president is not among these select elect of the kingdom?

Maybe, just maybe, we will soon enter a time when doubters and true believers can begin to sift through the pages of history and understand both the person of Ronald Reagan and the hunger of Americans for a super hero. The phenomenon of this man is unquestioned. His lasting place in history is still up for grabs. And what hunger must be abroad in the land for a god-figure to unite and inspire so many Americans. Why? What are the circumstances that propelled him into immortality and when can we expect another figure to capture this same hunger inside the American public?

My back yard adds to the mystery. The Easter lilies saved from Easters past came into bloom this week. They had obviously missed Easter and even Pentecost and I had begun wondering if they were waiting for the 4th of July. Do these Easter lilies know something I do not know? Are they among the true believers?

CHAPTER SEVEN

Let Your Life Speak

Politics in our nation is misguided. I have an extensive experience with the rise of Richard Nixon from his election to Congress in 1946 to his vice presidency to Dwight D. Eisenhower. I personally knew the people as he came to power, the methods and people used to defeat his enemies and reward his friends. The tragedy is the people whose lives were destroyed or severely damaged.

Richard Nixon was elected to the U.S. House of Representatives in 1946 using ruthless, immoral politics. He won the election against Jerry Voorhies who was considered by the press the most effective, capable, and knowledgeable representative in his ten years. And Nixon defeated Voorhies by deceit and tactics that were false, misleading, and paid for by Nixon. Nixon challenged Voorhies to debate. Voorhies never avoided a debate. So Nixon hired Hollywood actors to be at the debates. They were paid to heckle Voorhies and applaud Nixon. There was not a shred of evidence of the hecklers' lies. Nixon's people even employed some guys from Hollywood to attend rallies where Voorhies was speaking alone. These men would boo at Voorhies and call him a Communist.

Voorhies had a camp in Pasadena where young men needing help and guidance were given it. Ben O'Brien was one of them. He became an attorney and began his practice in California. He was instrumental in the events following the air crash in Pacoima that killed four boys. Ben O'Brien and his friends joined Reverend Hillary Broadus (his son being the Reverend William T. Broadus) with assistance building the hospital after the air crash.

Richard Nixon then ran for Senate in 1950 against Helen Douglas. She was one excellent leader, but she faced the same type of ridicule as Jerry Voorhies. My first wife's parents lived in East Los Angeles at the time and recalled phone calls relaying messages such as, "Did you know Helen Douglas is being supported by the Communist party?" It was a smear job—an immoral, unjust hack job by Nixon's paid people! They even advertised that Douglas voted fifty to sixty times with the avowed Communist congressman Mark Antonio. The only time she ever voted with Antonio was to answer "present!" during roll call.

The corruption continued with Nixon. In 1952, both Earl Warren and Eisenhower had run for the presidential nomination. The California delegation of Republicans was supporting Warren. Nixon used his friends to cook up a deal that would change their support of Warren to Eisenhower. Joe Holt was a candidate for the House of Representatives in Southern California in the congressional district where I lived. His father was a sponsor and friend of Richard Nixon. Lemoine Blanchard owned a lumber company in North Hollywood. Lemoine Blanchard's father was a close family friend. His father liked me, and he donated a large stained glass window when we built a new building at St. Matthew's. Joe Holt and Lemoine Blanchard were delegates to the Chicago convention. Members of the California Republican group, with Holt and Blanchard, headed for Chicago.

The delegation was trying to pull off a deal to have Dwight Eisenhower run for president with Richard Nixon as his vice president. They got off the train at Surmac, Illinois, and went to the Eisenhower headquarters where arrangements were made to change from support of Earl Warren. Earl Warren was livid when he found out. On nomination day, he was going to be double-crossed. Herbert Brownell, Nixon's manager for the deal and member of New York State Assembly, confronted Warren asking what Warren wanted for giving up without a fight. Earl Warren was granted his request. Eisenhower's first appointment after winning the presidency would be Earl Warren to chief justice of the U.S. Supreme Court, a decision he later cited as his biggest mistake because Warren was a liberal Republican. Herbert Brownell was attorney general in Eisenhower's cabinet. I heard Lemoine Blanchard who was a delegate to the convention in Chicago recount this story at an Optimist Club meeting in North Hollywood. It is a sad commentary on morals in our political system.

In 1964, Lyndon Johnson had Hubert Humphrey introduce civil rights legislation. Johnson relied on Hubert because Johnson was never a civil rights guy. Hubert turned to the group that had formed the

Democratic Farmer Labor Party and the ADA in Minnesota—me, Max Kampelman, and Walter Mondale included—asking us for suggestions. Once the legislation was written, Johnson had Hubert provide his liberal senators while President Johnson got enough Southern segregationist senators to support the legislation. Lyndon Johnson was from Texas. He never knew or wrote anything about civil rights. Johnson got the credit, which was all he wanted. The implementation of the legislation in southern states was a different story. In states and communities, many of the enforcers did not change their views. They winked, dragging their feet.

Group involved in passing the civil rights legislation

At age thirty-seven, Hubert became the first Democratic senator from Minnesota since before the Civil War. He was very successful. The congressional record contains ten pages of national policies, laws, and programs that Hubert was associated. A small handful of these are the following:

- Medicare
- Food for Peace Program
- National Defense Education Act
- Establishment of Arms Control and Disarmament Agency

- Nuclear Test Ban Treaty
- Peace Corps
- Food Stamps Program
- Job Corps
- Wilderness Preservation Act
- Head Start Program
- Establishment of Department of Housing and Urban Development
- International Development and Food Assistance Act
- International Security Assistance and Arms Export Control Act
- Humphrey-Hawkins Full Employment and Balanced Growth Act

Hubert Humphrey was nicknamed the Happy Warrior. He agreed with John Adams's description of politics as "the spirit of public happiness."

Hubert Humphrey became vice president to Lyndon Johnson in 1965. When Hubert was nominated to be vice president, he was told, "This is a marriage with no chance of divorce. I need complete loyalty." Lyndon Johnson was an imperial president. He was in full charge. Whatever he decided was what he got. All those in his control followed his orders, or they were in his doghouse and punished.

One of Humphrey's roles was to preside at the National Security Council in LBJ's absence. When Johnson was out of town, Hubert proposed a way out of Vietnam without more bloodshed. Around that same time, I was in Washington DC on hospital and Casa Loma College matters. I was invited to Hubert and Muriel's home at 17 NW Tenth Street for breakfast (back then they had no special home for the vice president). Greeted by Muriel, I noted she was depressed, not her bubbly self. Hubert was getting ready for his day.

While having breakfast, I noticed that Hubert also seemed down.

"Why are you so down in the mouth, Hubert?" I asked.

He said, "I presided at the NSC meeting in the president's absence. I made a proposal for getting out of Vietnam."

The council had approved. But Lyndon Johnson wanted to win the war in Vietnam. The Gulf of Tonkin event, which led the United States into the war, wasn't even a real event. It was phony except on paper. Hubert had tried to talk him out of it. Thousands of American troops were murdered or captured. Johnson wanted a victory. He told Hubert he could never let him preside at the meeting again.

Hubert then said to Muriel, "I can't be mad at the president. He is so nice to you."

Muriel was quick to respond to Hubert, "That is not the question. He has no reason not to be. But what he has done to you is unforgivable."

Eric Fromm once said, "The lust for power is not on strength, but on weakness." A lot of politics is not on strength. A lot of politics is getting people on your side that can do things. Lyndon Johnson said of Humphrey, "Hubert's problem is that he trusts his enemies too much." The Happy Warrior saw the best in people. Hubert was torn between his loyalty to the president and his conscience, his personal friendship and his political responsibility. He originally supported Vietnam but changed his view over a short period. He sent a personal memo to the president warning against escalation of the Vietnam War.

Nineteen sixty-eight (1968) was a tragic election year. Hubert contributed to his own defeat because he publicly embraced President Johnson's Vietnam policy. (Humphrey also had other "war issues." He failed his military physical numerous times, one time from a hernia. Neither war supporters nor war protestors trusted him!) HHH was at war with himself. "You can never be tough enough when you have to prove your masculinity."

During his 1968 bid for the presidency, Hubert's problem was he had a constituency of one—please President Johnson. Hubert was made candidate when Johnson decided not to run for president again after Eugene McCarthy won a primary. Johnson gave his resources but never endorsed Humphrey. The humorist Tom Lehrer was devastating:

> Whatever became of Hubert
> Has anyone heard anything?
> Once he shone on his own
> Now he sits home alone
> And waits for the phone to ring?

Humphrey succumbed to President Johnson and became a hatchet man. Johnson betrayed what Humphrey's people wanted. Johnson controlled the campaign. He decided where Humphrey would campaign and what would be in the speeches. I call it the betrayal of Humphrey.

The 1968 Democratic National Convention in Chicago was a catastrophe. All of Hubert's friends tried to get the location and the dates changed. There would be violence. But Johnson and his friend Mayor Daley ruled with the same imperial "what I want is what I'll get" style as Johnson.

The convention was a stormy mess for both the delegates and the protestors. Hubert initially gave public support of Vietnam, and the antiwar protestors had not forgotten. People were brutalized and arrested. I was there from California. Even in the hotel where many stayed, protestors dumped human waste on each other.

Humphrey was still nominated amid all the confusion.

Hubert had an aversion to fund-raising. His civil rights and his commitment to peace were his number one priority. He always got an explosive response, but he never escaped the controlling president. The imperial controller president still kept the lid on Humphrey. Johnson never let Hubert be his own man in the campaign. Perhaps Hubert would be elected, but I didn't believe it possible without a break from Johnson. I advised my friend as such.

Three weeks before the election, I got a phone call from my friend. Hubert was going to be liberated. He was doing a speech free to be Hubert. I met him at the NBC studios in Burbank. I told him it needed to be sooner. It was too late. Richard Nixon won. I have been unable to find out what deal, if any, there was between Nixon and Johnson.

As he closed his campaign for president, Hubert eloquently said, "I have always believed that freedom is possible. I have believed that the basic decency within this nation would one day enable us to lift the veil from our eyes and see each other for what we are as people—not black or white, not rich or poor, not attending one church or another, but as people standing equally together free of hate or suspicion."

AMEN!

Hubert wrote me after his loss. "I am ever grateful for your generous assistance and I'm terribly sorry that I didn't do better. It is always a disappointment to lose but it even becomes a more painful experience when I realize how disappointed my friends and supporters were.

"I am going to concentrate my efforts in the Senate. I believe I can do a good job there for my country and for the things in which we both believe. I welcome your advice and counsel and indeed need it. I look forward to your continued friendship and support. Let me hear from you."

And he kept his word. In 1978, he was successful in the passing of the Humphrey-Hawkins Full Employment Act (coauthored with Congressman Gus Hawkins of Los Angeles). This bill provided the following:

1. The right to profitable, creative employment, profitable not only to the individual but to the community

2. The right to an adequate standard of living
3. The right through collective bargaining to a substantial share in the management of industry
4. The right to security against the hazards of unemployment, accident, illness, and old age
5. The right to the maintenance of health
6. The right of leisure and its effective use

On reflection, Hubert had a career in progressive issues—trying to make a great society. He supported civil rights, federal aid to education, Medicare, job corps, the food stamp program, vocational aid and welfare.

Hubert had a sense of humor about himself, which is the most important characteristic of a *real* sense of humor. He took a lifetime of ribbing about his being late—usually the result of stopping to talk to a child or a person who wanted to ask him something. Hubert never used humor as a weapon, although he would help people laugh at themselves without a barb.

One incident is illustrative. I had gone to Mesa, Arizona, to dedicate Mesa Lutheran Hospital, which I helped to organize and was administrator of for a short time. On the platform that afternoon was Senator Barry Goldwater. In the course of my address, I talked about Project Hope and my involvement with it through Senator Humphrey. Project Hope is a program bringing medical care to poor areas of the world. At the reception following, which was hosted by a friend of Hubert's, Senator Goldwater handed me an envelope and said not to open it until I was making my pitch that evening. He said, "It'll surprise them." It was a check for Project Hope in the amount of $500. (You see, he had to support this liberal program because his wife was involved.) The newspapers in Arizona and Los Angeles printed the story and someone sent Hubert a copy. Following is a letter that Hubert sent to Barry Goldwater:

I am pleased to note that you made such a generous contribution to Project Hope. We are going to make a liberal out of you yet. You are slipping. But don't resist—keep coming. You are too good a fellow to waste your talents. It's time to revitalize the conservative wing of American politics.

Best wishes for the new year.

Sincerely, Hubert H. Humphrey

No wonder Barry Goldwater said that he could trust Humphrey to be president.

People often chided me when I have said Hubert was a humble man. Obviously, I did not mean he was an Uriah Heep or Caspar Milquetoast. He was teachable, and he learned from both professionals and ordinary citizens. He had more ideas for meaningful change in public policy than anyone I have ever known. Hubert was open and responsive to learning and listening and discussing ideas with every person he met. He believed, "Life is too serious to be taken solemnly."

A gift from Hubert Humphrey

I enjoyed having fun with him. He was everybody's friend. He was interested in you. Both he and Muriel came out to Casa Loma College. He was always interested in you. And he cried. Hubert wanted to be loved. He was unable to be cruel. He was always impulsively outgoing and spontaneous. And he was lonely. Despite all the legislation he supported to help those in need, he said, "There is no law that I can get passed that can cure loneliness."

Hubert always lacked money to live on. He had, through a friend, established a blind trust in a mutual income fund that grew to a million dollars by the time of his death. The money was for Muriel, their four children, and their ten grandchildren. So, after all, he died a rich man.

Hubert Humphrey died January 13, 1978. Vice President Mondale said, "He taught us how to hope and how to love, how to win and how to lose. He taught us how to love, and finally he taught us how to die."

Excerpt from "I Ran for Mayor"
From *Campus Lutheran*

There are many lessons that I learned as a candidate that I didn't learn when I was a leader or worker for someone else. When the spotlight is on you, the feelings are quite different than when you are out of the limelight.

We are living in a period in which men's reputations are ruined or marred by irresponsible smear artists. Accusation is tantamount to guilt. Exploration of new ideas is forbidden. Conformity is loyalty. Circumstances condemn. Past experiences are unforgiven and never forgotten.

Emotion Rules

Words betray, for our language is so limited. Every word carries with it not only the objective meaning but also overtones of emotion. When a minister, for instance, uses the word *strict*, it means something entirely different than when the same word is used by a doctor, lawyer, or businessman. Or take the word *reform* in the emotional context of the minister who uses it and the citizens who hear it. Inject this objective and emotional problem of words into the arena of politics at all levels, and you have a problem that democracy has yet to solve.

Emotion rules even among the so-called intellectuals. Party platforms have little or no influence on voters. Speeches change few votes. The support of a prominent person or an organization doesn't move the voters appreciably. Even political machines, except in primaries for local office, do not swing elections. Getting on the bandwagon of the supposed winner is not very important. The fact is that it is deeds and events that decide elections. It is the feelings of people toward the events that move them or that further solidify their decisions.

During my campaign, I had more mail, more sympathy, more emotion stirred up by the fact that my children had the mumps than by all the attempts I made to consider the vital issues of administrative and legislative reform. Likewise, it was the firing of the police chief who had said he supported my candidacy that turned the tide in the general election. The issues and the personal qualifications of the two candidates played little or no part in the final decision at the polls.

Following closely and related to emotion is the place of rumor, which has been a tool in politics for centuries. In the campaign, there was a rumor about me for every person who needed a rumor to justify his decision to vote for me or against me. As a minister, I was a natural target. They couldn't miss. I was "kicked out of my church," I was "a nigger lover" (president of the Urban League board), I was "the kikes' candidate" (chairman of the state FEPC), I was "anti-Catholic," I was "anti-Swedish" (I am Irish, and my opponent was a Swedish immigrant), etc. Since my own campaign, I have watched this rumoring technique work on others. I am alarmed by it.

Not All Black or White

Yet the compromises that are a part of life are even more a part of seeking public office. Thus it is that many political scientists insist that "democracy is the art of the impossible." There are many 51, and not 100, percent decisions. Life is not all black or white: it is full of grays. Because this is so, the American political system is possible; but also it is always in peril.

I cannot pass by without commenting on the influence of the media of communication, especially the press. Regardless of your partisan political allegiance, you must admit that we are victims in most American cities of a one-party or single-point-of-view newspaper situation. Every objective study, like the Nieman report, reveals statistically that in approach, in coverage, and in handling of news, this is the case in almost every major city in this country. And the interlocking ownership and control of other media of communication such as radio and television by the same persons who own our newspapers is not only true but frightening in its portents for democracy.

My experience and observation leads me also to a conclusion that applies to the special case of the Christian minister. There is an anticlerical feeling not always voiced but nevertheless operating in the lives of our people. In part, it is based on the false distinction between the sacred and the secular. We ministers have helped foster the heresy that we are of a different order and class than laymen. The laymen have come to believe us. Yet the early life of our country indicates that the clergy were active in all areas of living, especially in government.

The previous analysis may lead the reader to conclude that my experience was all negative. Nothing could be further from the truth, though I believe it is important to see that side of the picture clearly if we are to remedy our errors and weaknesses.

Rich Rewards

I was richly rewarded in many ways. I made friends of all races, colors, creeds, and ages, all degrees of educational level, economic standing, social position, and political complexion. You simply cannot appreciate the strength of democracy until you have seen people give their time, talent, treasure for your cause without any thought of reward. The kindnesses expressed in a myriad of ways by hundreds of people were reassuring and rewarding.

"A man should pray for the privilege of seeking public office," it has been said. I had this privilege. This was a noble experiment whose overtones reached far and wide. Issues of vital concern were crystallized. People were awakened, involved, and strengthened in their concern for local government, which needs strengthening more than any other governmental level.

CHAPTER EIGHT

Nonviolence or Nonexistence

Peace means so many different things to so many people. To men it simply means the absence of war. As long as there is injustice and conflict between husband and wife, between employer and employee, between black person and white, between those who have and those who have not, there cannot be peace.

The peace we seek moves with gentleness and pleads in loving example. It is a preventative task that—when it sees poverty, injustice, hate in any circumstance—seeks to rectify because it knows that this is the cause of the wars, which destroy men and nations. We hate war, and we desire peace, but we no longer assume the choice is ours.

The fallacy and weakness of our political system is that the leaders are their own authority as to what is a just cause for violence. It is said that Billy Graham got George Bush to accept Jesus as his personal Lord and savior. Neither George Bush nor Dick Cheney is saved. They are wrapped up in a belief system that justifies what they want. The U.S. Constitution holds the words "Promote the general welfare." Replace the term *general* with *specific*.

When George W. Bush was going to war against the Taliban, Billy Graham was invited to the White House to spend the night, and was used to bless the war. "There comes a time when we have to fight for peace." Billy left out that the fight would require killing the enemy. He has offered prayers that approved Vietnam, Kuwait, Afghanistan, and Iraq. He has never apologized for those. Jesus did not endorse "holy wars" or "just wars." God does not sanction religious violence to achieve peace.

Peace Points, a resource series offered by Lutheran Peace Fellowship, offered the following explanation of the "just war" criteria:

1. The war must be a LAST RESORT. Every effort at negotiation and arbitration must have been tried.
2. The war must have a JUST CAUSE—to protect the innocent and defend against unjust demands and threats of force.
3. The war must be waged by a LEGITIMATE AUTHORITY.
4. It must be FORMALLY DECLARED.
5. It must be fought with PEACEFUL INTENTIONS. It cannot be waged by a crusade mentality, self-interest, or pride, but must be for the well-being of all people.
6. There must be a reasonable HOPE OF SUCCESS. The goals must be achievable without squandering the life and property of the people.
7. The means used must be PROPORTIONATE to the ends sought. War mustn't cause unnecessary destruction that outweighs the final good the war seeks to achieve.

The list continues with the humane treatment of prisoners and mercy shown to and assistance provided for the defeated group. I can't think of an example. If America goes to war, the other people are wrong. America suffers financially (and emotionally) at home while individuals in our military and others in business are seeking peace and justice abroad. I get confused as to what we're really suffering. We all do.

George Bush lied to us about weapons of mass destruction. Our people and our country's resources have been sacrificed in the sands of Saudi Arabia and the Persian Gulf. We were lied to for the "special welfare" of oil companies, war weapons—manufacturing companies, and S and L's. John Mitchell said "follow the money" about Watergate. I say "follow the money" in the political arena at every level.

This is about Domination by those in power. Money is power, and power is over control. We seek control of people's lives. During World War II, Executive Order 9066 took the property of the Japanese Americans and put them in camps all over the country. The justification was different than Naziism. The United States wanted to catch spies. The reason was the same—fear and hatred. Fear becomes hate. It corrodes, corrupts, and becomes cancerous. It lashes out to destroy. It no longer sees another human as a person but as an object, an it. No spies were caught by EO 9066. The

U.S. government made a load of money selling property "acquired" during this process. I met the head of Japanese American resettlement. We did a lot to help.

In Minneapolis during World War II, I was a conscientious objector. I still ministered from a distance to the seventy to eighty young people from my parish that joined the service. In the Twin Cities, we were always doing something to strengthen our witness. The Board of Social Missions sent a letter to every Lutheran pastor and congregation (there were about eighty in the Twin Cities!) requesting every pastor and every member of the congregation to give at least five dollars to fund a ministry to men who were conscientious objectors.

Two pastors at the meeting had a harsh exchange and objected to giving the money. When I urged my brothers in faith to contribute, a pastor from St. Paul got up and said he "wouldn't give a dime for those yellow bellies." And he continued his harangue. He was followed by another pastor who was going to give five dollars and presented his case for conscientious objectors even though he himself had a son in the air force.

I finally closed the discussion and said I was going to give my five dollars. And I remarked I was going to give five dollars for the pastor that wouldn't do it. About a year and a half later, shortly after the surrender of Japan on August 15, 1945, to end the war, we had another meeting. The man who said he wouldn't give five dollars for conscientious objectors asked his colleagues to forgive him for what he had said. He had not contributed his five dollars, but he made an interesting confession. The other pastor who had defended us thanked him, and we had a prayer.

Most violence occurs when an individual or group decides on something that others do not believe or want. Then a decision is made to make others believe we should have whatever it is for America. One of the four groups to come out of the leadership of the Fellowship of Reconciliation is Amnesty International. They have opposed torture. Under the hysteria of patriotism, we have allowed declared suspects to be subject to torture. I can't reconcile this with anything Jesus said about anyone.

The war in Iraq is a war we chose. It was not of necessity. So the cost in dollars and in lives will be the legacy of the born-again religion, which takes no responsibility for the deaths. Nationalism embraced by Billy Graham (also Jerry Falwell, Pat Robertson, and other groups trying to make a theocratic state) seeks to outlaw abortion and gays and lesbians while violence spreads through the rapture, Armageddon, the death penalty, and war.

War is oppression at home. The largest numbers of our soldiers come from communities of five thousand or less, poorer communities, young people drawn in to military service with the promise of money through grants. We forget that the United States is not the god in this world, or the representative. We send out our young and our poor (with hopes of respect and money) to be our military might to control people's resources that we want. Our soldiers return psychologically damaged, many dependent on government resources.

Unfortunately, violence takes many forms—rules, regulations, laws, and reforms that restrict people from being humans. For example, it is economic violence when corporations do not pay a living wage. We have a war on crime, a war on poverty, and a war on terrorism. The mistake is that the enemy must be defeated rather than loved and transformed. We have many enemies, many wars, within America. We have yet to treat our own people humanely.

As governor of Texas, George Bush was responsible for allowing twenty-six executions (in one case the defendant was sleeping during trial and was still put to death!). Every western Democracy except the USA has abolished the death penalty. Only one out of one hundred convicted murderers are sentenced to death, and conviction depends upon your race, economic and social class, your age, geographic location of the murder, etc. Above all, conviction depends upon whether you have any money! No millionaires on death row, only minorities.

Robert Kennedy, in a speech he made a few days before his assassination, said, "Whenever any American's life is taken by another, unnecessarily, whether it is done in the name of the law or in defiance of the law, by one man or by a gang, in cold blood or in passion, in an attack of violence or in response to violence—whenever we tear at the fabric of life which another man has painfully and clumsily woven for himself and his children, the whole nation is degraded."

Why don't we feel secure if military might can fulfill its promises? Does executing one person make us safer? We have the most highly developed industrial strength, the largest navy, the greatest stockpile of atomic weapons. Yet the feeling of insecurity is more epidemic since the end of World War II than at any time within memory.

We live in a fearsome time. Within forty-eight hours, every living thing can be exterminated. I was invited to Harriman, New York, elected by the Board of Social Missions on the Church and Economic Life to be part of a discussion of peaceful uses of atomic energy. Twenty-five of us—labor leaders, clergy, and scientists—met for three days. The scientists shared that with nuclear energy, we have the know-how to take 150 acres in the center of the country to produce all the fruits and vegetables that we at that time consumed in the United States—a large hothouse. The technology is there, but the idea never had any strength in any political parties.

There are many peaceful uses of atomic energy. Instead we have more nuclear weapons than any countries combined (and people are fighting for food!). It is tough to deal with our need for energy, an energy crisis of our own making. But it is the result of our own distorted priorities. All nuclear tests, no matter how tiny the weapon, are acts of hostility against all mankind. Where is our conscience?

The greatest anxieties arise not from politics or diplomacy, but from dark passions and deep-set prejudices. Among them is the spirit of hate with a fear from which there often seems no escape. It is fear of the uncertain, the unknown. We can't know if we will be bombed tomorrow. We aren't sure if the Hispanic guy walking toward us is a thief ready to raid our pocket. We don't know why a man wants to marry another man. But we have these misunderstandings and fears that turn into hate and violence.

Any human problem is an opportunity, not a disaster. It just requires hope. It requires letting go. It requires letting go of those personal prejudices. John Shelby Spong, a retired Episcopal, wrote the following titled *A Manifesto! The Time Has Come!*:

> I have made a decision. I will no longer debate the issue of homosexuality in the church with anyone. I will no longer engage the biblical ignorance that emanates from so many right-wing Christians about how the Bible condemns homosexuality, as if that point of view still has any credibility. I will no longer discuss with them or listen to them tell me how homosexuality is "an abomination to God," about how homosexuality is a "chosen lifestyle," or about how through prayer and "spiritual counseling" homosexual persons can be "cured." Those arguments are no longer worthy of my time or energy. I will no longer dignify by listening to the thoughts of those who advocate "reparative therapy," as if homosexual persons are somehow broken and need to be repaired. I will no longer talk to those who believe that the unity of the church can or should be achieved by rejecting

the presence of, or at least at the expense of, gay and lesbian people. I will no longer take the time to refute the unlearned and undocumentable claims of certain world religious leaders who call homosexuality "deviant." I will no longer listen to that pious sentimentality that certain Christian leaders continue to employ, which suggests some version of that strange and overtly dishonest phrase that "we love the sinner but hate the sin." That statement is, I have concluded, nothing more than a self-serving lie designed to cover the fact that these people hate homosexual persons and fear homosexuality itself, but somehow know that hatred is incompatible with the Christ they claim to profess, so they adopt this face-saving and absolutely false statement. I will no longer temper my understanding of truth in order to pretend that I have even a tiny smidgen of respect for the appalling negativity that continues to emanate from religious circles where the church has for centuries conveniently perfumed its ongoing prejudices against blacks, Jews, women and homosexual persons with what it assumes is "high-sounding, pious rhetoric." The day for that mentality has quite simply come to an end for me. I will personally neither tolerate it nor listen to it any longer. The world has moved on, leaving these elements of the Christian Church that cannot adjust to new knowledge or a new consciousness lost in a sea of their own irrelevance. They no longer talk to anyone but themselves. I will no longer seek to slow down the witness to inclusiveness by pretending that there is some middle ground between prejudice and oppression. There isn't. Justice postponed is justice denied. That can be a resting place no longer for anyone. An old civil rights song proclaimed that the only choice awaiting those who cannot adjust to a new understanding was to "Roll on over or we'll roll on over you!" Time waits for no one.

I will particularly ignore those members of my own Episcopal Church who seek to break away from this body to form a "new church," claiming that this new and bigoted instrument alone now represents the Anglican Communion. Such a new ecclesiastical body is designed to allow these pathetic human beings, who are so deeply locked into a world that no longer exists, to form a community in which they can continue to hate gay people, distort gay people with their hopeless rhetoric and to be part of a religious fellowship in which they can continue to feel justified in their homophobic prejudices for the rest of their tortured lives. Church unity can never be a virtue that is preserved by allowing injustice, oppression and psychological tyranny to go unchallenged.

In my personal life, I will no longer listen to televised debates conducted by "fair-minded" channels that seek to give "both sides" of this issue "equal time." I am aware that these stations no longer give equal time to the advocates of treating women as if they are the property of men or to the advocates of reinstating either segregation or slavery, despite the fact that when these evil institutions were coming to an end the Bible was still being quoted frequently on each of these subjects. It is time for the media to announce that there are no longer two sides to the issue of full humanity for gay and lesbian people. There is no way that justice for homosexual people can be compromised any longer.

I will no longer act as if the Papal office is to be respected if the present occupant of that office is either not willing or not able to inform and educate himself on public issues on which he dares to speak with embarrassing ineptitude. I will no longer be respectful of the leadership of the Archbishop of Canterbury, who seems to believe that rude behavior, intolerance and even killing prejudice is somehow acceptable, so long as it comes from third-world religious leaders, who more than anything else reveal in themselves the price that colonial oppression has required of the minds and hearts of so many of our world's population. I see no way that ignorance and truth can be placed side by side, nor do I believe that evil is somehow less evil if the Bible is quoted to justify it. I will dismiss as unworthy of any more of my attention the wild, false and uninformed opinions of such would-be religious leaders as Pat Robertson, James Dobson, Jerry Falwell, Jimmy Swaggart, Albert Mohler, and Robert Duncan. My country and my church have both already spent too much time, energy and money trying to accommodate these backward points of view when they are no longer even tolerable.

I make these statements because it is time to move on. The battle is over. The victory has been won. There is no reasonable doubt as to what the final outcome of this struggle will be. Homosexual people will be accepted as equal, full human beings, who have a legitimate claim on every right that both church and society have to offer any of us. Homosexual marriages will become legal, recognized by the state and pronounced holy by the church. "Don't ask, don't tell" will be dismantled as the policy of our armed forces. We will and we must learn that equality of citizenship is not something that should ever be submitted to a referendum. Equality under and before the law is a solemn promise conveyed to all our citizens in the Constitution itself. Can any of us imagine having a public referendum on whether slavery should continue, whether segregation should be dismantled, whether voting privileges should be offered to women? The time has come for politicians to stop hiding behind unjust laws that they themselves helped to enact, and to abandon that convenient shield of demanding a vote on the rights of full citizenship because they do not understand the difference between a constitutional democracy, which this nation has, and a "mobocracy," which this nation rejected when it adopted its constitution. We do not put the civil rights of a minority to the vote of a plebiscite.

I will also no longer act as if I need a majority vote of some ecclesiastical body in order to bless, ordain, recognize and celebrate the lives and gifts of gay and lesbian people in the life of the church. No one should ever again be forced to submit the privilege of citizenship in this nation or membership in the Christian Church to the will of a majority vote.

The battle in both our culture and our church to rid our souls of this dying prejudice is finished. A new consciousness has arisen. A decision has quite clearly been made. Inequality for gay and lesbian people is no longer a debatable issue in either church or state. Therefore, I will from this moment on refuse to dignify the continued public expression of ignorant prejudice by engaging it. I do not tolerate racism or sexism any longer. From this moment on, I will no longer tolerate our culture's various forms of homophobia. I do not care who it is who articulates these attitudes or who tries to make them sound holy with religious jargon.

I have been part of this debate for years, but things do get settled and this issue is now settled for me. I do not debate any longer with members of the "Flat Earth Society" either. I do not debate with people who think we should treat epilepsy by casting demons out of the epileptic person; I do not waste time engaging those medical opinions that suggest that bleeding the patient might release the infection. I do not converse with people who think that Hurricane Katrina hit New Orleans as punishment for the sin of being the birthplace of Ellen DeGeneres or that the terrorists hit the United Sates on 9/11 because we tolerated homosexual people, abortions, feminism or the American Civil Liberties Union. I am tired of being embarrassed by so much of my church's participation in causes that are quite unworthy of the Christ I serve or the God whose mystery and wonder I appreciate more each day. Indeed I feel the Christian Church should not only apologize, but do public penance for the way we have treated people of color, women, adherents of other religions and those we designated heretics, as well as gay and lesbian people.

Life moves on. As the poet James Russell Lowell once put it more than a century ago: "New occasions teach new duties, Time makes ancient good uncouth." I am ready now to claim the victory. I will from now on assume it and live into it. I am unwilling to argue about it or to discuss it as if there are two equally valid, competing positions any longer. The day for that mentality has simply gone forever.

This is my manifesto and my creed. I proclaim it today. I invite others to join me in this public declaration. I believe that such a public outpouring will help cleanse both the church and this nation of its own distorting past. It will restore integrity and honor to both church and state. It will signal that a new day has dawned and we are ready not just to embrace it, but also to rejoice in it and to celebrate it.

I have made this manifesto mine.

CHAPTER NINE

Catechism on Nonviolence

We live in a domination system. The domination system locks oppressed people against each other. It offers a spiral of violence. I do not believe Jesus was born of a virgin or that he walked on water, turned water into wine, or passed through walls in postresurrection appearances. Jesus's purpose was to enlighten and expose. He was a heretic.

Raine Eisler describes a more ideal lifestyle, one that more closely matches Jesus's way of nonviolent love and the mission of the Fellowship of Reconciliation. She calls it the "partnership way." Partnership ways reject ranking. Partnership, according to Eisler, suggests that life is a web that supports living things rather than a pyramid in which someone, thing, or idea is higher, or on top.

Under no circumstances can one person dictate to another. Marriage and all relationships are about partnership. There is no escape for any man or woman from having a relationship with all men and women on this earth. Partnership in every area is the goal, and the road to partnership cannot be decided by males alone or by a salvation formula. I joined the Fellowship of Reconciliation after my first year of seminary. The FOR emphasizes forgiveness as the heart of reconciliation.

Forgiveness *is* at the heart of everything. It begins with the person who has been forgiven. Once I have been forgiven, I need to be forgiving. Look at Nelson Mandela, Bishop Desmond Tutu, and the Truth in Reconciliation Committee. The guilty had an opportunity to talk about what they had done. When Mandela was released after twenty-seven years of wrongful imprisonment, he did not dwell on vengeance. The Commission tried to find out where there was any willingness to repent, to forgive—the road to partnership. The idea was not to punish, but to forgive and be rewarded in the community.

We need to be involved in seeking partnership, in bridging the gaps between others. We need to develop organizations that strengthen nonviolence like the YMCA and the ACLU. Schopenhauer wrote, "Compassion, concern for others is the basis of morality." Empathy, feelings with others, is the key to healthy relations with other people. These twin ideas of compassion and empathy enabled Pacoima Memorial Lutheran Hospital to be unique and different in the quality of patient care we have given in healing the whole person.

Good health is more than just plumbing. And partnership begins with our relationship to us—body, mind, and spirit. In addition to Casa Loma College that trains nurses, I had plans to open Golden State Community Mental Health Center. We secured $100,000 to be raised at a dinner chaired by former California governor Edmund G. Brown. The plan was for a twenty-six-bed wing to the hospital operated by the hospital board. Governor Brown said, "Community mental health centers provide treatment and care near the homes and close to places of work. Without these centers, we would have to assign mental health patients to tax supported institutions, thus taking them away from their homes, their loved ones, and their jobs." Pacoima Memorial Lutheran Hospital was to be concerned with every person physically, mentally, and spiritually.

Governor Edmund Brown with myself and Carl McCraven,
CEO of Hillview Mental Health Center

On February 9, 1971, an earthquake struck the San Fernando Valley. I was rudely awakened at 6:01 in the morning. The hospital was destroyed in forty-five seconds. Three other major hospitals serving the area, Olive View, LA County Hospital, and San Fernando Veterans Hospital were also destroyed. The day after the earthquake and evacuation, the general hospital wing of Pacoima Memorial Lutheran Hospital was declared so severely damaged structurally that it would have to be demolished.

Before the quake hit, there were four hospitals and fifteen hundred beds serving the medical needs of two hundred thousand area residents. The community had needs. Within five days of the earthquake, we opened a twenty-eight-bed emergency room (in what was supposed to be the new mental health center) despite city, state, and federal regulations. Whenever a regulation went against the efficient, concerned, and compassionate care of people, I ignored it. I didn't care even if I went to jail. Nearly three hundred patients were helped each day by the virtually heroic loyalty of nurses, physicians, and aides.

I took on the leadership to secure rebuilding funds for the hospital. Congressman James Corman met with Warren Dorn on a plan to seek legislation to amend a law passed in 1970 regarding funding for hospitals destroyed in the floods in Texas. This bill would help PMLH get the funding it needed. The legislation worked its way through Congress and was to be signed by President Nixon.

Robert Finch, the special counselor to President Nixon and former lieutenant governor of California, called Warren Dorn to let him know that Caspar Weinberger was going to recommend a veto. Dorn, Finch, and Corman suggested I go to Washington to meet with Weinberger to persuade him to change his mind. I agreed and went to the White House. I waited in a room with the young man who was bringing the information to justify the decision for the veto.

After my meeting with Weinberger, I caught my plane and called Warren Dorn. He said, "President Nixon owes me a big favor." He also said counselor Finch knew all about it. The favor was this: when Nixon was defeated for governor of California by Pat Brown, he had few friends left in the Republican Party. But Warren Dorn organized a gala financial party. Nixon was grateful. So Warren Dorn and Robert Finch persuaded Nixon to sign the bill. He did, and I was given the presidential pen used to sign the bill. I still have it.

Events decide the direction of our lives. I watched Luther Youngdahl, governor of Minnesota, light the torch to hundreds of straitjackets and leather wristlets while over a thousand patients in the Anoka State Hospital cheered themselves hoarse. That event, in retrospect, inspired me to devote myself to the humane treatment and prevention of mental illness. That event led to a succession of events and experiences and expectations too numerous to name here.

The hospital was reopened, and the building and rebuilding continued. Within six months, we returned the hospital to its prequake level of 110 patient beds. We were operating at a huge deficit, but the amazing thing was that we were back in the business of serving the greater good of the community. The president of a synagogue in Encino, California, said to me, "I don't believe in Jesus the Messiah, but if you want to live the way He did, I'm on your side." That is the message of Jesus as I understand it.

I don't think we should give up on anyone. Society must find every person with a problem. I have been involved with organizations trying to do just that. Beyond finding individuals in need of help, society must do more than give a man a fish. If the community is to be served, it must teach a man to fish.

Hillview Mental Health Center (the final result of the dream of Golden State, which originally opened in 1966 at PMLH) is still growing and serving the mentally ill in the San Fernando Valley. The mission of Hillview Mental Health Center is "to help empower individuals and families affected by mental illness by assessing their needs, strengths and goals and then working collaboratively with mental health professionals to plan services that are person-centered, culturally competent and effective in promoting recovery and the ability to live as participating members of their community."

Additionally, "Hillview Mental Health Center's programs were shaped by the economic and social realities of the communities we have served since 1966. Some of the lowest income, ethnically isolated areas in the county are in our service area, where families are dealing with high unemployment, substandard housing, lack of resources for health and mental health care, lack of transportation, and poor education. As of 2007, little has changed." As of today, these challenges still exist.

Why does Hillview persist? What good are we doing? I don't always have the answers I want, but the following letter of thanks from a Hillview client dated 2007 should answer these:

> I was thinking about the difference between where I was a year ago and now. The Difference is thanks to the charity that Hillview

has shown me. Last year, I was a shattered and abused homeless woman living in the dirty space between two industrial buildings. I lived like an animal. I was being harassed because I was vulnerable. Even other homeless people picked on me, attacked me and stole from me. Men degraded me with words and actions. I couldn't call the police because they wouldn't help a homeless person. I was afraid, alone and losing my mind.

I was seeing a therapist once a week trying to pull out of a deep depression that led to my homelessness, but as long as I remained residentially challenged that was impossible. I tried to find a place to live but resources in Los Angeles County were stretched thin.

One hot summer day, the harassment, abuse, fear and lack of sleep became too much. I felt that I had reached the end of the road and that road stopped at a set of railroad tracks. I prepared myself by getting drunk and taking a whole bottle of pain pills. The sun beat down on me but I had gone cold inside. The echoes of people's taunts and hatred rang through my head. I literally heard voices telling me that I was worthless. As a train approached I cried out one last prayer, "Forgive me, Father" and then I laid my head down in front of the train. The engineer blew the whistle stridently. I even heard him shout "Get up" in a panicked voice. I closed my eyes and prepared for impact, ready for the inevitable mercy of death.

The train hit my head with a tremendous slam but did not crush me. Instead I was pushed off the tracks. In minutes, paramedics were there. I called out, "Don't save me. I don't want to live!" Then the blackness enveloped me.

I awoke in a hospital room. I was very sad and disappointed. I felt around for my head injuries. The back of my head wasn't cracked open. I was surprised by that. The pain was excruciating. But I was alive. By some miracle, I had survived a freight train to the head.

However, that didn't mean I was happy to be alive. Quite, the contrary. I was feeling angry that I hadn't planned my suicide better. I questioned why God prevented my death, then started wondering at God's purpose for my life.

I stayed at UCLA Harbor Hospital for 30 days. Doctors were extremely kind to me. I was given an antidepressant every morning. My mood improved. Every day I was able to do a little more. A social worker placed me so I wouldn't end up back on the street.

That's where Hillview comes in. I was admitted to their Urgent Care building where for 30 days I was protected from the world. Positive thoughts actually came to me. I wondered if maybe I did have a future at all.

I qualified for Hillview's AB2034 program as an at-risk person because of my criminal record. I had been arrested twice; something I was deeply ashamed of. But my criminal record proved a godsend here. The goal of that law is to prevent homeless people from repeated arrests or hospitalizations due to their mental illness. A safety net for those lost souls who have fallen through the cracks in the system.

That day in July when I thought I had reached the end turned out to be the beginning. And this new hope was possible because of Hillview. Without them I merely would have been treated at the hospital, given a month's supply of medication and turned back out into the mean streets. Instead of languishing in filth and degradation, I have been listened to, cared for and assisted toward a better life. I am getting help through counseling, group therapy and psychiatric care. The days when I feel suicidal and depressed are getting fewer. I am now going to school and making plans for my future. I look for reasons to live. Hillview did that for me.

In 2002, renovation of the Pacoima campus, which houses the Mentally Ill Offenders program was complete. I was honored by the naming of the new wing—Rev. John G. Simmons Opportunity House—housing mentally ill clients sent to Hillview instead of prison. At the dedication, I was introduced by my friend and fellow activist Ed Asner:

I am honored to join you today as we celebrate the newly remodeled and expanded Opportunity House which from this day forth, will be known far and wide as the Rev. John G. Simmons Opportunity House. As Dennis McCarthy so beautifully wrote in his Daily News article, "John Simmons has spent a lifetime illuminating the darkest corners of our society."

As most of you here today know, the object of this 24 year old Mentally Ill Offenders (MIO) program—simply put—is to restore independent living skills for recently incarcerated mentally ill people with the intention of a successful transition back into the community. Essentially, it's designed not to waste people.

People who enter the MIO program are assisted in developing better coping skills to avoid further incarcerations, further substance abuse, hospitalization and criminal behavior. This inspired program provides structured day and evening services that include individual therapy and group counseling in a home-like setting to aid transition back into the community. Before leaving the program, clients are assisted with where and how they will live and support themselves, including how to find ongoing services . . . Wow! As a senior citizen in America, I no longer know where and how I will live. I could use that kind of help. Where do I sign up?

This enlightened approach certainly makes more sense than the usual thinking that locks the cell door and throws away the key. As Clarence Darrow put it so well, "You can only protect your liberties in this world by protecting the other man's freedom."

The perfect description of how Rev. John Simmons has led his life (he certainly has been a hero to me) is that wherever a battle was being fought for justice and humanity, there he was.

I was on the original committee that put together LA Family Housing. LA Family Housing's main purpose is to provide meaningful assistance for the homeless in the way of a private home (not a shelter) and a community. LAFH provides more than housing. It requires employment search and job training, life skills training, money management and mandatory savings

Ed Asner, myself and Bethene at a Sunair event

program, parenting classes, tutoring and homework assistance, healthy meals, medical and mental health services, drug and alcohol counseling, homebuyer education, and more. *Every* health issue is addressed.

After the earthquake, I was invited to a meeting by the board members of an organization called Sunair Home for Asthmatic Children. I joined the board. Sunair started in 1958. Seven Jewish men were looking for a place for their sons, all who had asthma. Asthma was disruptive of a child's schooling as it required trips to the hospital. Asthma became a more serious problem with increasing smog in Southern California. Sunland/Tujunga was considered a smog-free area, so the founding members of Sunair bought a home there. They called it Sunair Home for Asthmatic Children.

Children with asthma went to school and lived at the Sunair Home. They were able to get the treatments they needed at the Sunair Home. Sunair raised money by connections with people in the movie industry. Sunair continued until the early 1980s when the necessity of emergency room treatment for asthmatic children decreased drastically due to more effective medicines. The property was sold.

Sunair still serves the community it served at its start. The proceeds from the sale of the property went into a fund for Sunair. Of about one and a half million dollars invested through places, Sunair gives up to $160,000 a year to kids programs in Los Angeles. Sunair supports asthma and allergy camps

Sunair Board

(requiring on-site doctors) and children's programs in minority communities. Sunair gives regularly to MEND, Meeting Every Need with Dignity.

Excerpt from the DEDICATION ADDRESS
(by John G. Simmons, administrator) of Hillview Mental Health Center:

This event embraces a never-to-be-repeated experience of joy and satisfaction. This event is the birth of expectations.

The experiences that produced today's event are many and varied, individual and familial, institutional and community. Life's seemingly insignificant experiences are meaningful. For instance, last week a poster was prepared announcing today's event. The painter was apologetic, "I omitted the word 'mental' before Health Center." "I'm pleased you did—that highlights a significant truth of my experience."

HEALTH is Wholeness. Health is Organic. Health is Salvation. Salvation is Health. When we are healthy all of the physical, mental, spiritual, political, economical, and social parts of our lives are functioning as one . . . as a Whole. We have too long experienced what the fragmented, isolated, piecemeal, separated, segmented Health Care System has done to undermine and destroy the ecological nature of man's health. Our experiences have been that we have not been able to keep up with the health needs of people, nor have we been successful in preventing the increase of illness in our society because of this anachronistic approach to health.

Our experience at PMLH indicates that health care for all illnesses and diseases that afflict people can be treated more adequately in a community general hospital. We have experienced that going to where people live in the community is a healthier approach than merely confining them in large impersonal institutions away from their loved ones and their community.

Our experience has taught us that a healthy person must have the continuing opportunity to participate in decisions affecting his life; that a healthy person must have the opportunity to learn from his experiences, including his mistakes and failures and must have the opportunity to develop his own resources and skills to deal with his problems. We have experienced the truth that every

110

person has problems but that at certain times they cannot solve them by themselves. They need help. We must be prepared to make help available.

We have had a very small inadequate inpatient facility, but this has been helpful to us. The presence of a Mental Health staff improves the patient care of all of the patients in the hospital. For instance, the obstetrical patient who develops a psychotic reaction following the birth of a child can be helped. Or the surgical patient who becomes depressed following surgery can be helped. We have provided consultation in the innumerable psycho-physiological diseases discovered in many patients. We have discovered that follow up care can be most helpful to patients not specifically admitted as "Mental Health Patients."

We have also experienced that we can provide consultation for patients who come to PMLH through an emergency, suffering from different traumas as a result of accidents, alcoholism, drugs or attempted suicide. We have experienced the need for rehabilitation with patients who show no apparent visible scars.

This event today is filled with expectations. Many of them fall when they are frustrated by the resistance of other people or by the happenings of life. We are people of hopes. Our hopes move us today for creating a more meaningful tomorrow.

We expect that during the months of the building of this facility that more and more persons within our family and within our service community will become aware and informed and educated concerning Mental Health, as well as the relationship of Mental Health to Health.

We hope to create a healthier environment for all the people of our community, rather than molding people to fit into their unhealthy environment. We too often send people back into the same environment that forced them into the hospital in the first place. We usually behave as our "environment" tells us. We must seek to prevent Mental Illness and to teach Mental Health. This means meaningful work is needed for all persons. This means adequate housing, adequate diet, and adequate space for the recreation of our lives. Poverty follows the diseases of the Heart and Cancer as the third major cause of death.

We have environmental pollution which makes a livable environment for healthy living difficult and death premature. The pollution of air and water, the atmosphere, the misuse of land, the lack of adequate public transportation, and the noise which destroys our environment must be attacked vigorously if we are to effectively use the facility we construct here. The facility is important, but more important is the program of services that are rendered to people, where they live and work, to prevent illness and disease. We must avoid the Edifice Complex as well as avoiding institutional multiple sclerosis.

Disease and sickness affect both rich and the poor. Prosperity and Poverty both produce their own diseases and illness. Health is now a promised right for all our people and not merely the privilege of the favored few. We expect that all of us working together will make it possible for the promised right of health care to be realized right of all people in our community.

I invite you to give your hands and hearts and minds and all your resources to the achievement of our expectations for this Community Mental Health Center.

CHAPTER TEN

The Voice of Hope

In a sense, the hospital failed. I could blame plenty of people. The government didn't give us money, for example. We needed $900,000. The hospital doors closed in 1986. We almost lost the mental health center also.

I ran for Congress in 1986 and 1988. These attempts at public office could also be seen as failures. I ran against someone who had been in office for twenty-five years. On record, he never introduced a bill that passed. He was a nice guy. He was always good for a vote for those who got him in office, and he showed up to "things." He was very conservative, a John Birch guy. Come will or come woe, his status was quo, as the saying goes.

I knew I wouldn't win, but I did some important things. (That is the essence of the hospital. To be a true failure, it would be insignificant to the community. Casa Loma and Hillview Mental Health Center still remain.) I proposed a highly publicized plan that I called a Marshall Plan for the USA (Ed Asner and others raised money and awareness for my campaign). With Miles Clark, I wrote the following printed in *Plowshare Press* in Spring 1988 (vol. 13, no. 2):

> In Cologne, Germany in 1949, we watched dusty gray coated Germans scrape bricks that would rebuild their nation with our help. Europe was emerging from a time of despair.
>
> Between 1947 and 1952, that war-torn continent received $13 million from the United States in one of the most unique programs

of international cooperation for reconstruction the world has ever seen.

The seed of the Marshall Plan aid enabled Europe to rise from the ashes until it became a community of nations of economic and moral vitality, of peace, health, and a high living standard unmatched almost anywhere.

The Marshall Plan used five factors to make it work: a concept, cooperation, a process, financing, and caring.

It took the combined efforts of dedicated governments, organizations, and individuals to achieve. We look back at the Marshall Plan as the one proof that equal amounts of charity, cooperative thinking, hard work and patience can pay off.

Can it work in America? Will a Marshall Plan USA do for us what the original did for Europe? Can we rebuild America? Does it need rebuilding?

Clearly, the crystal ball sees hard times ahead for America. The conventional and exceedingly pessimistic wisdom of this election year says: don't worry if your favorite presidential candidate loses, the party that wins the White House will be inundated by a deluge of problems, long swept under the rug.

We must now face that mountain of imperative challenges, the greatest array of this century, most of which we brought upon ourselves no matter who the President. Trillions of dollars are desperately needed for long overdue repair of our infrastructure: broken bridges and highways, mass transit and solid and hazardous waste facilities now decrepit, public buildings dilapidated, to name only a few urgent concerns.

We need funding for our public schools (faltering beside our economic competitors) and for health care for every member of every family (we have the least effective health care in the western world). We also need to deal with displaced and dislocated workers, the underemployed and the underpaid.

Emergency is the way to describe the needs of our industry, our eroded lands and our farms, our failure to stamp out drug use (there would not be a supply if it were not for our colossal demand for drugs)? These are just the most obvious of our nation's problems.

Can the Marshall Plan work here? Yes!

Why dredge up an old idea like the Marshall Plan? It is worth exploring because it was a powerful and dramatic idea that was practical and successful. It is one of the few plans that worked a clear-cut multi-faceted dynamic program for the nation, for regions, for counties and cities, even villages. So why invent a totally new idea when we can redesign an historic, almost legendary, plan that worked, adding our own original and innovative fine tuning for the 1990's and 2010?

I have been told to park my religion at the door to the public arena—that religion is a private affair. If the issues of morality, justice, war, peace, and love are private affairs, then that is not the God of love. The idea that God saves you by sending Jesus to die for your sins is irrelevant. This abandons Jesus's way of nonviolence and love.

Jesus was crucified for living in love with all people—a way of living in morally embracing justice, peace, and love. Eighty-two times, Jesus said, "Follow me." Not once did he say, "I am the second person of the Trinity." Jesus was a pacifist in practice, not just in words.

When we seek to live in love, we live and love in the beloved community. We do not submit to the power of God but to the power of God's love. We are a community of hope. We are the hope of the community. Hope is an essential, necessary part of the structure of life and of a man's spirit, a companion to life and growth. But it can only be meaningful in community.

Tennyson asks, "What is it all, if all of us end but being our own corpse—coffins at last. Swallowed in Vastness, lost in Silence, drowned in the deeps of a meaningless past?" Hope is not passivity, not resignation, not worship of the future, not primarily otherworldly. All of these attitudes are disguised forms of hopelessness born of a lack of love for life.

The world of humanity is sick. Millions are in the winter of despair. The youth are not sure that they have a future. Adults feel hopeless because they feel so helpless. They feel powerless in the face of a bureaucratic society, the dehumanizing of the individual.

Our hopes have been shattered. Promises have been broken. Our dreams have been blasted. The results are strewn everywhere—hardening of the heart snuffing out empathy and compassion; withdrawal in bitterness, cynicism, and fatalism; the aggressive search for self-sufficiency. We have become self-destructive or destructive of others. Presently, hope has gone out of a lot of people's lives. If you have no hope, you don't give a damn what you do and to whom you do it!

We have a problem always of what can we hope—what do we hope for? We hope for a better life, better conditions among those closest to us. We have hope for people who mean something to us. Hope is not vacuous—it is not "if you are good, then you get into heaven." (It is more important to get heaven into you!)

Where is heaven? I know where hell is right now—it's other people! People don't always do what they're supposed to given the opportunity. But do I believe I am going to be coming back? Or living in some sort of eternal bliss? I'm still struggling with that one. What's going to be left when I leave? We want to believe that we can somehow take it all with us. We justify our selfishness desires. The truth is difficult.

Hope comes from letting go. That means there are certain silences. When a person is silent at a funeral, for instance, what are they hoping? Literalists think of heaven. It is unpleasant news if a person thinks it is all over when it is over. Heaven doesn't always seem to answer the question, though, so we're silent in the presence of death. We cannot know what happens to us after death—it's hard to process, so we ignore it.

Silence is a response to feeling helpless. We place our money with banks because we are guaranteed to get it later. There are no guarantees in death. We move over to the silence that becomes denial, avoidance of the issue. Wondering what's going to happen is not reassuring. People hope for things that have no reality. Underneath, we are hopeless, empty.

What is going to be left? Nothing personal. Not my prejudices, my poor attitudes, my misguided desires, my selfish needs. Nothing but what I've done for other people. I've been guided by the four organizations that came out of the Fellowship of Reconciliation: American Civil Liberties Union (ACLU), Doctors Without Borders, YMCA, and Amnesty International.

Most of my life was given in the church trying to do as the Fellowship of Reconciliation.

So I come to the end of my life without losing the way, Jesus's way. Is there any hope for others? I don't see very many signs. I have no hope of the change in our world community in my lifetime. We have no hope with a system that is hierarchical. My hope is to stop arguing over irrelevancies. It is all irrelevant except our relationship to others. Hope should be for a more loving relationship with all people. Forgiveness is the key. Forgiveness keeps life connected.

Forgiveness begins with the person who has been sinned against. It is followed by reconciliation. The Principles of Reconciliation are the following: 1) forgiveness comes from the person who has been offended, 2) reconciliation, 3) reconstruction and rebuilding of the relationship occurs. Then justice comes. Then we come to peace.

The reality is churches may be guilty of making evil worse. Church leadership has been "come weal or come woe, our status is quo." Insisting on certain ideas such as creationism and school prayer is detrimental to community. The Fellowship of Reconciliation, if taken seriously, will force a new idea of the church—fellowship of persons facing problems human beings face rather than fellowship of persons believing improvable ideas. All the flourish and doctrinal stuff is not going to make the church what it ought to be.

We have to find a way to respect each other's beliefs and still work together. Every person of any religion—Christian or not—has the drive to find a higher being. That being guides their behavior. We have to face our divisions. Bishop Spong claims denominations are counterproductive and destructive. I agree. Denominations are not universal. There are only five major world religions.

Many religions come with a certainty I cannot accept. It matches fundamentalism. Fundamentalism is the embrace of biblical literalism. Fundamentalism believes in Armageddon. People believe that Jesus will return some day soon to end the world—the Rapture. Not only is it a bad idea, but it is a useless idea. It makes God out to be a tinkerer. Fundamentalism is wrong scripturally and practically. We move from deeds and actions in the world to a belief system.

We are biblically illiterate. We call the Bible "the Word of God." Such an assertion assumes that God is a very humanlike being who has the ability to speak to a particular people in a language that they understand. That claim cannot endure. What did Jesus write? Nothing. The Bible is based on oral tradition, the first Gospel written years after Jesus lived. The problem with oral tradition is that it is easily distorted. The context changes over the years as the story is passed down. God works through flawed human beings, and flawed human beings wrote the Bible.

In all the encounters I've had with fundamentalists, they fail to see the humor in the Bible. Think about Jonah and the whale—a man living inside a whale. (There is a comedy skit titled *A Whale with a Bellyache*. Jonah discovers he's not alone in the whale's belly. Jonah meets a writer doing research on man-eating whales. Jonah also meets a Food and Drug Administration bureaucrat checking on whale food.) The Bible has some very interesting ways of humor, mainly because it deals with some very difficult subjects. In the book of Jonah, God changed his mind. Really?

The Bible addresses universal, timeless themes of relationships to groups, to your family, to your community. Alternatives to current worship are needed in all religions. I cannot restate enough times that I come with more questions than answers. We have to move toward a theology and worship and global plan of action for people. New hymns. Challenge communion. Abandon the idea of substituting Jesus on the cross (or any belief) for your inaction. I attended worship services with the Fellowship of Reconciliation. Creation was affirmed, but not as a zoo. God is a creative spirit of love. God is not a person. He is personal.

We will have to have a church that is primarily concerned with emphasizing that humans are part of a community. We need faith that embraces everyone. The church also has to grow up in terms of understanding scripture. Groups are divisive. We have to become partners.

The journey from me to *we* is a long one. Almost all of our time is spent trying to satisfy our own five senses. Hope is an inner active readiness for what can be the reality but what may not now be the reality. Hope is a decisive element in personal or relational change. Hope is aliveness and awareness to others in community. Hope is love in action.

The hope that I have relates to the ability of the community to realize that we are responsible for looking out for and helping each other. The community has got to get rid of war and violence. I cited violence as the greatest problem (threat) to humanity. It is not easy being a pacifist. If someone came in and started to attack me, should I lie down? At what point do you have the right to resist? Is it a violation of FOR?

I've tried to live on the growing edge of biblical/theological understanding. Living on the edge means you don't have many answers, you have many questions. I can't get a handle on human folly—why we act the way we do toward each other. I hope that we can come to a realization that there are enough food and resources for everyone if we get over "me first."

What hope do I have for criminals? I would hope that society would get them to a place where they could return to society. I don't think we should give up on anyone. I don't believe in the death penalty. Only thirteen states agree. It is not directed toward rehabilitation. Even to the guilty, it does not solve the problem. It does not deter crime.

I'd hoped we would have a major change in our leadership for a long time. Now, with Obama, we have that. Barack Obama is not the incapable optimist he is made out to be by the media.

What is my hope? That more people will seize the opportunities to bridge the gaps that are dividing us. Hope can only be meaningful in community. Our common unity is in God. That's why we worship. Our hope is our faith in God's promises, God's acts, God's activities—all of these are His life in us and His mercy toward us. We are saved through community, not in individual isolation (denominationalism creates isolation).

We are bound in the bundle of life with the Lord our God. We are to gather the scattered, bind up the wounds of separation. We are to hold the world together. We are to unite what has been broken and fragmented. Our hope can only be realized when it finds expression in acts that weld us together in community. The most healing and healthy experience is to participate in the reshaping of the community. That is what I worked for in Minneapolis and in Pacoima. That is why I have lived to see what I have seen. Your life should be an expression of your willingness to give up your life.

Excerpt from "Forgiveness and Reconciliation"
July 22, 2007
Reverend John Simmons

This sermon is entitled "FOR—Forgiveness and Reconciliation." This is the essence of our job, our task, our opportunity. God forgives you. By grace you are saved through faith. Nothing you can do earns God's forgiveness. No one can give it to you. God gives it to you, by grace. That's the essence of what Luther had to say. He made a lot of mistakes in other ways but the words "By grace you are saved through faith" is the essence of the Gospel.

But, just coming to receive the bread and the wine or receiving God's assurance of His forgiveness through grace, you have a responsibility to repent of that which caused the sin, and sins that you commit, I commit. The penance involves changing your ways, a transformation, a taking a hold of the thing that's obsessed you and caused you harms and harm to others, your sin, you have to change your ways. We don't pray to change another person's ways, that's their problem. You can encourage it but you can't do anything about it.

But when you manage to understand that after forgiveness begins repentance and change in your attitude and your lifestyle. That alone can lead to reconciliation with that which destroyed your relationship in some way—with another person, with the environment in which you live, with the people you associate with and people that are not of your immediate association but people of the world.

Not retaliation, you seek to make peace through reconciliation. It is called agape, which is a love word. It's the toughest one. It means exactly what I said in the beginning that God's grace saves you, nothing else.

Forgiveness is from strength. It begins in remembering, not in forgetting. Not over our weakness. No resentment. When we forgive, we are free. Forgiveness is the response to anger and hostility. Forgiveness is more than a second chance. "Forgiveness is seven times seventy," as Jesus said.

Without forgiveness and reconciliation, politics is dead, violence continues, conflicts continue and war continues.

War is violence and forgiving each other requires patience but above all it requires love without violence. And war is a place and now is a time and place for repentance. God has forgiven us. We repent, change our ways and seek reconciliation with the enemy or enemies. War is nothing but slaughter.

The moral truth is that lies, half truths, deceptions need exposure to the light. The war against the poor, or races, or classes begins with forgiveness if there is to be any reconciliation. When we surrender our power over to other people and share power with them and for them. Only then can reconciliation result.

Forgiveness, repentance, reconciliation, that's our worldwide responsibility, but it begins with us. Amen.